Mum, is that a human being or an animal?

A book on Autism

by

Hilde De Clercq

ISBN 1 904 315 06 2

Published by Lucky Duck Publishing Ltd

www.luckyduck.co.uk

Commissioning Editor: Barbara Maines
Editor: Mel Maines
Designer: Barbara Maines
Illustrators: Philippa Drakeford, Helen Weller, Gemma Stone

Reprinted Sept 2004

Printed by Antony Rowe Ltd.

First published in the Netherlands in 1999 by Houtekeit – Antwerp.
ISBN 90 5240 511 5
Mama, is dit een mens of een beest?

"Greetings, keeper of the herd,
Over there, on the side of the road,
What is the wind whispering to you?"

"That it is the wind and that it is passing by,
That it has come before,
And it will come again,
And what is it telling you?"

"It is telling me much more,
It tells me many things,
Memories and sadness,
And about things that have never been."

"You have never heard the wind.
The wind only talks about the wind.
What you have heard is a lie,
And the lie is within you."

Fernando Pessoa

Acknowledgements

For Freek,
who, through hail and storm, cycled
to make overhead transparencies for me.

For Jeroen,
who is so patient with the 'darling'.

For Liesbeth,
who helps and knows Thomas inside out.

For Rutger,
who knows why.

With many thanks to Theo Peeters for his support and to
Kees Rood who assisted me in writing this book.

The photographs used in this book have been chosen to illustrate the
text and are not pictures of Thomas.

Contents

Foreword

This is the kind of book that should be written more often. Sometimes we learn something new through personal experience, something which up until now, has not been the subject of research. This time, it is how 'thinking through details'' works in an autistic child.

When I heard Hilde talk about her son's 'thinking through details'' or 'local coherence', almost a synonym for 'weak central coherence', at a conference a few years ago, I immediately recognised it as a new and important breakthrough. I remember telling the audience, "This is an interesting point, but you must first have in-depth knowledge of autism."

"In-depth knowledge?" replied Hilde. "But, it is precisely through this 'thinking through details' that I have always been able to explain my son's autism."

In her notes, I read the following recollection: Thomas waves at his grandfather only if he is in his green car, never if he is in a car of another colour. The same holds true if the car turns left, he waves. If it turns right, however, he does not wave. I asked Hilde to continue her research on this theme and it was tested for the first time in Skive, Denmark, during an international conference gathering of one thousand participants. I still recall some of the reactions.

Marie Bristol, former TEACCH colleague and presently head of 'American Autism Research' (the CPEA) in Washington, stated, "I have never heard anyone explain the world and life from the point of view of a person with autism as clearly as in Hilde de Clercq's presentation." Yannick Beyer, director of the Brondagerskolen for autism in Copenhagen, said, "For years we have been talking about the importance of visual back-up for people with autism. After this presentation, we finally understand a bit better what they really see."

Since then, Hilde has been holding conferences on this topic. Sometimes, parents and professionals don't immediately recognise this ''thinking through details'', but they always come back to it. "Yes, many of the issues we were not able to pinpoint previously, have to do with 'thinking through details'."

You can't always find what you are looking for. An issue must first have a name. In this little book, issues are given a name and, therefore, they become recognisable.

In the workshop on parent-professional collaboration, I often hear Hilde say, "Listen to what parents tell the babysitter about their child. Generally, you will find examples there of 'thinking through details'."

Gunilla Gerland, author of 'A Real Person', and a person with autism herself, has also encouraged Hilde to continue her research and write a book. Gunilla especially appreciates Hilde's respect for Thomas' thought process. All too often we find that educators try to 'eliminate' it or try to adapt it to our way of thinking. That is often the price we pay for that great idea, 'integration'.

After having read, 'Mum, is this a human being or an animal?', V.A., another woman with autism, wrote, "Sometimes a detail that seems insignificant leads me to locate and check certain things and events. This allows me to reach a level of understanding and the possibility of a concept which, in turn, will lead me to the real content. Detail is my first stronghold, a landmark for my way of thinking, analysing and determining. Whether the detail is important or not is something I can only find out once I've reached the level of understanding, and not vice-versa. I relate to what Hilde De Clercq writes about Thomas. I have been down the same path. I think through details and still today, in any situation with new data, I follow the same mental route as I have always done, from the beginning."

"My relationship with Thomas," said Hilde, "has truly and strongly shaped and determined my life and my awareness. He would present me with an enigma and we would figure it out together. My experience living with him is the key to this book. In fact, this book should be called Thomas' book, because it is not mine, it is his. It is a homage to him."

If ten people cover their eyes, touch an elephant for a few seconds then describe their experiences, each will probably describe a different part of the animal's body. But the person who describes its long trunk or its ivory tusks will make the animal more recognisable than the person who focuses on the left foot. Autism can also be explored in different ways. The person who tries to understand autism through 'thinking through details' will have a sound basis for understanding the syndrome and also for treating people with autism. This is why, 'Mum, is that a human being or an animal?', is a must for anyone involved in the world of autism. This is no exaggeration. Read it.

Theo Peeters
Director
Centre of Training on Autism
Antwerp Belgium

A fundamental notion:
over-selectivity in people with autism

"I didn't understand why my sister suddenly disappeared in the daytime. Kerstin had always been there before and now she no longer was. As my visual impressions were very clear and sharp, I connected whatever happened with what I could see. To me, everything boiled down to what I saw and sight was the most reliable of my senses. It was as if my sight was tangible.

I desperately wanted to understand and this led to theories: if everything looked a certain way in the living room, the sun shining in through the curtains, the ashtray on the table with a newspaper beside it and if Kerstin then came home from school, I thought that everything had to look exactly the same the next day, for her to come back from school again. It quite simply had to be like that. And in fact, it often was...

People often disturbed my theories. Just when I thought I had grasped the connection between things, someone would move the newspaper and I no longer knew what to think. Would Kerstin not come home now? Couldn't she come home? Ever again? Or didn't I understand anything? In that case, was everything else I thought also quite wrong? No, it must be that my sister couldn't come home until everything was put right again. The newspaper had to be back in its place – that must be it. If it wasn't like that, everything I believed in and knew about was invalid.

There was no flash of magical thinking in all of this. On the contrary, it was all immensely concrete. What I saw was what happened, neither more, nor less. On these occasions, when my theory was sabotaged by things not turning out as I'd anticipated, I had to start on a new one. There had to be some way of understanding the world."

Gunilla Gerland (1996)

From birth, children are looking for meaning. Ordinary children soon look to the invisible, the hidden meanings of things. They go 'beyond the information given', Bruner (1974). They feel intuitively that the meaning behind the perception is more important than the literal perception itself. That is their hypothesis, their theory and with their hypotheses and observations, they learn the abstract and subtle meaning of language and social behaviour. Meaning is what counts.

Children with autism start out with somewhat different theories and hypotheses. Not that the search for meaning does not exist, but it happens differently and painfully, Frith (1987). Perception is dominant and sometimes details prevail in the maze of perceptions, details they select and put together to find a meaning in this confusing, sometimes chaotic world, of the invisible, of meaning not directly perceived.

To illustrate this concept, we should mention one of the many studies made on perceptual dominance, the experiments of Schuler and Bormann (1980). Children with autism had no difficulty in doing a sorting exercise based on visual similarities using identical objects, i.e. black plastic combs, objects that look alike, a small red plastic car and a brown metal car, broken objects and whole objects, a broken clothes pin and a new one. However, it became more and more difficult for them as the criteria based on perception were reduced and similarities in meaning increased, i.e. a part of a whole, matching objects with a functional complement, like a comb and a wig, matching an object with another having a similar function, like a comb and a brush. Perception remains overwhelming in the development of meaning in children with autism.

The experiments of Schuler and Bormann give an idea of the unusual difficulties autistic children have in developing concepts. Studies by Menyuk and Quill, (1985) give an insight into their problems with early language acquisition. When ordinary children first learn the word 'chair', for example, for a short while they use 'chair' for anything upon which they can sit, i.e. a stool, an armchair, a couch. Their understanding goes beyond the literal perception, the 'invisible' meaning overrides.

During the first stages of language learning for children with autism, you will often see the opposite. If the word 'chair' represents a specific object, then you cannot use the word 'chair' for a bigger thing on which we sit, or for one of another colour, since the outside signs of recognition are too different. While ordinary children 'over-generalise', children with autism seem to have specific difficulties with spontaneous generalisation.

Bronowski and Bellugi (1970) state similar facts about the process of language acquisition. An ordinary child uses the word 'chair' for a specific chair. The child may associate the word with many other kinds of furniture, but listening to his parents speak about chairs, he begins to limit the use of the word to one particular kind of furniture that we describe as chairs. All chairs have the specific quality we could call 'chair-hood'. But there is no exact definition of chair in terms of colour, size, etc. Yet we know that children with autism need precise definitions because of their difficulty with thinking abstractly.

It does not seem hard to imagine that in order to identify an object one has never seen before as a chair, one must ignore many of the qualities of individual chairs. Instead, one must limit one's criteria to certain aspects, such as:

- ◆ a movable seat made for one person
- ◆ a back rest and four legs.

In other words, the definition of a chair includes specific functions. We take into account not only what we see, but also its use. Fay and Schuler (1980).

Children with autism seem to be over-selective. It is easier for them to give a very concrete label than to grasp all the rules linked to understanding. One particular aspect of perception can come to dominate and play a role in early development. In the following chapters, I will focus mainly on and give examples of visual over-selectivity.

Take my son, Thomas. Before he could even see, he had already selected a smell, my perfume, and had given it, in our opinion at least, too much importance. He was only a few days old when he first started to react in an unusual way. I was breastfeeding him. I discovered if I changed my perfume, he would refuse to drink any more. It was no mere capricious refusal, he was hungry, he was losing weight and he was furious. It became a matter of life or death. When I had the right perfume on and held him tight, he was a peaceful, easy baby. With any other perfume, my little Thomas was unmanageable. I didn't understand it at all, but that's the way it was.

Six weeks later, when he began to see, similar things happened. I always had to wear the same sweater. My hair had to be tied up in a ponytail with a red bow; I had to wear the same earrings (when you take a baby in your arms and it puts its head on your shoulder, the first thing it sees are the bow and the earrings). Years later, when he could speak, he'd often say, "Put on your tail." Much later, when he had understood that his Mum would still be his Mum even with other earrings, other sweaters and with another hair-do, he'd be very happy to see me wearing those first earrings. Then I would be 'my nice Mum'. If I didn't wear my blue sweater, or have my hair tied up with a red bow, or didn't wear the same earrings, even if only one detail was missing, his world seemed to fall apart. For him, Mum was a set of details that went together and nothing could be changed.

This apparently was the way it worked: if one detail changed, clearly the whole thing changed. How could that be? I began to understand that Thomas handled information and thought in a different way. Little by little, I tried to respect his way of thinking as much as possible and to adapt to it, for better or for worse; but his kind of thinking didn't have a name yet and remained quite disturbing. This lasted for years. Now he understands that Mum with another perfume is still Mum and that Mum without her red bow is still Mum. He has good learning abilities and continually evolves, but his way of understanding often works through details first.

I hope this book will clearly explain how 'thinking through details' influences understanding and concept development in people with autism and the role that over-selectivity plays in their communication, their understanding of social behaviour and their imagination. Here are just a few anecdotes to give you an idea of the effect of my son's over-selective thinking:

> I signed Thomas up in his new kindergarten and met with the teacher and the psychologist. I remember saying, "If I had come here in my pyjamas to talk to you he wouldn't have noticed, but I don't even want to think what his reaction would have been if I had been wearing different earrings!"

> It is late. His father has the night shift. Someone rings the doorbell. I'm taking a bath and the children open the door. Concerned and curious, I get out of the bath and listen from the top of the staircase to see who is there. Then Thomas opens the door into the hallway, sees me stark naked and cries out, frightened, "You don't have your ponytail on!"

> Thomas is twelve years old. His father has just shaved his beard and moustache off without telling anyone. Thomas goes into the bathroom and runs out immediately. "Mum, someone's sitting in our bathtub!"

I could go on and on, for his whole life seems to be a series of similar situations. For example:

- He trusts blondes with ponytails like Mum.

- He avoids his dad when he changes his after-shave lotion.

- Grandpa is only welcome if he wears his reading glasses.

- How happy we were when Thomas waved goodbye to his grandparents when they left! But I soon realised that he only did so when they were in the green car (he went through his green period, his red period...).

- Grandpa comes back from the barbershop. A tantrum, "I want you to have your hair cut long again."

- Will he creep into bed with his Mum? Yes, but only if she has her long purple T-shirt on.

When it appeared that Thomas had autism, I began to read like mad because I wanted to understand him better. In the literature on autism I found here and there the so-called interest in detail, but only as if it were just another arbitrary aspect of cognitive development. Occasionally though, I found a few examples that made me think of Thomas and this was very important for explaining some of my child's 'strange' behaviour to me.

> "He didn't like to kiss his Mum. His little body would grow rigid each time she tried. It was much more fun to turn saucers round and round. People were so difficult: they said and did so many things he didn't understand. But objects, you could count on them, they had their own place, they didn't do unexpected things. His dad would always say, "Look over here," or "Say daddy for once," but the little boy didn't understand a thing and instead looked at the way the light filtered through the curtains. And much later, when he saw the same kind of light filtering through his father's hair, he suddenly said, "Say daddy for once." "He can talk, he can talk," cried his dad who went and got his Mum. "Say it again, say daddy." But the little boy did not understand, since the light had disappeared once more."

Theo Peeters (1986)

A little boy sees a light and associates it with 'say daddy'. The words have nothing to do with the meaning, but rather with the perception of a visual detail.

I found a breakthrough in the understanding of 'thinking through details' much later when I read an article written by an adult with autism.

"For instance, when I am confronted with a hammer, I am initially not confronted with a hammer at all but solely with a number of unrelated parts: I notify a cubical piece of iron within its neighbourhood a coincidental bar-like piece of wood.

After that I am struck by the coincidental nature of the iron and the wooden thing resulting in the unifying perception of a hammer-like configuration.

The name 'hammer' is not immediately within reach but appears when the configuration has been sufficiently stabilised over time. Finally, the use of the tool becomes clear when I realise that this perceptual configuration known as 'hammer' can be used to do carpenter's work…

…Each step of these successive integration-phases does pose a considerable effort upon me, it's a type of effort that can best be described as 'thinking in the background'.

For me, to perceive something is equivalent with constructing an object using explicit trains of thought.

In fact, it should all be done in a fully automatic way without conscious effort and in rapid progression.

The autistic sensitivity for parts in the perception instead of wholes is common knowledge and is denominated as 'over-selectivity'."

Van Dalen (1995)

Donna Williams describes her 'thinking through details' in a similar way. She goes on to say that so much of what one perceives must first be decoded, like a piece a paper.

"The decoded information, 'white and flat and thin and square with a smooth surface', becomes interpreted into the recognition that what has been 'seen' is 'a sheet of paper'. The deeper processing for significance requires further internal messages to be sorted and relayed. Significance tells me what to do about paper: I need some of this to write on."

Donna Williams (1996)

The functional aspect comes after the perception at the very end – that you can write on it. People with autism must translate everything they perceive until they reach its function. In normal development, understanding is immediately linked to function and the two aspects are present simultaneously.

Just like Thomas, Van Dalen and Donna Williams are extremely sensitive and, in particular, too sensitive to details – having to put many details together before they can form a whole. It takes a lot of mental strength to build wholeness.

I ask an ordinary child, "How can you tell that this is a bird?" The child looks at me, as if to say how can you ask such a silly question. "Because it flies, of course."

I ask Thomas the same question. "How can you tell that this is a bird?" Thomas (very seriously - I must stress this point because many people who don't know autism think he has a sense of humour) says, "First I look and see if it is a person, or an animal. Once I know it's an animal, I look and see if it has four legs or two. If it has two, it's a bird."

A human being or an animal. I think back to a time many years ago, when we were on a streetcar. By then, I had taught him how to sort pictures well: these are the people and these are the animals. He knew how to do it perfectly. That afternoon on the street-car, he noticed a woman with a very strange hair-do and in his straightforward way, he said loudly, pointing to the lady, "Mum, is that a human being or an animal?"

Today, now that I know a bit more about over-selective thinking, I am sure that the lady's curly hairdo (a detail) reminded him of a sheep.

Part 1

Understanding

Autism is a pervasive developmental disorder which involves impairments in the qualitative development of what is also known as 'the triad':

- ◆ verbal and non-verbal communication

- ◆ understanding of social interaction

- ◆ imagination and play.

In the literature on autism, this triad is explained in various ways. I would like to explain it by using Thomas's 'thinking through details', which I will develop in this section in the next three chapters.

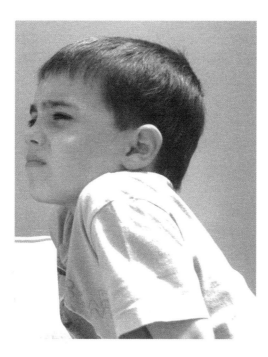

Chapter 1

Thomas and Communication

*"For a long time, I also felt very uncertain about what was meant by
food when you thanked someone for it. Was everything you ate
food? Should you say the same when someone offered you an
apple? What was food?*

*There were things that certainly were food – sausages were food
and meat was food. Was soup food? Soup was liquid. If soup was
food, then perhaps tea also was food? Though there were solid bits
in soup and there weren't any in tea. But what about porridge?
How could you use that phrase when you weren't certain what
food was?"*

Gunilla Gerland (1998)

*"...The appearance of the first generalised concept, such as
'furniture' or 'clothes', is as significant a symptom of progress as the
first meaningful word."*

Vygotsky (1994)

Thomas's early verbalisation kept me busy; it was so special and
peculiar. He could sing back whole phrases of Mozart's Requiem,
repeating Give me hope, Johanna, or saying over and over again
sentences like, "Of course, we can also try a combination of the two,"
but I knew only too well that he didn't understand any of it. I really
wanted to teach him how to talk, how to say simple things and ask for
them. In other words, how to communicate. I'd turn the pages of
books with him, giving names to pictures, but unfortunately, Thomas
didn't repeat anything.

About this time he walked around everywhere carrying a can of
tomato paste. So, I thought to myself, if he wants to say something,
surely he will talk about his can and from this, he'll learn to speak
about actual things, which is probably easier than talking about
pictures. So I showed him the can and suddenly, at last, he said,
"Thecan." It had worked; he would learn how to speak. I felt
encouraged. He would now also be able to learn other words, like
cookie or apple.

Well, it worked and it didn't work. It worked because he would repeat the words. But he didn't seem to understand them. Above all, he continued to call the can of tomato paste, 'thecan'. I must have said, "What do you want? The can?" and so for Thomas 'thecan 'was a word. And 'thecan' meant a can of tomato paste.

It was that simple. There were also days when I doubted his motivation and his goodwill. He could easily name thecan, cookie, bottle and apple, but sometimes he would seem to have forgotten the last word. I was sure he knew it and little by little, I began to lose patience. Day after day, every time I laid an apple in front of him, nothing happened. There were only two possibilities: either he had forgotten what he had learnt, he had forgotten the word apple, or he didn't want to say it.

One day, an apple fell off the fruit bowl. Suddenly I heard Thomas say, very clearly, "Apple." Apple! Did he say apple? So he does know the word. I was overjoyed. I waited for my husband's return. I took an apple from the bowl and asked Thomas, "What is this?" No reply.

"But he said it earlier. I heard him clearly. He said apple."

"Did he?"

Those were tiring days. Had I really heard it? Was I hallucinating? Some people thought I was overdoing it. "Just don't talk to him, eventually he'll come and ask you for what he wants." And yet, I persisted. "Thomas," I said, "What is this? What is this?" The questions were beginning to make Thomas anxious and were bringing no results. Much later, when I had nearly forgotten the apple business, Thomas's brother Jeroen came home with an apple in his hand, which he had got at Sarah's birthday party. Thomas saw the apple and said, "Apple." Suddenly something clicked in my head. Jeroen had a green apple in his hand. The first apple had been green as well. I took a few green apples and asked, "What is this? What is this?" This time they were all apples. So, for Thomas, apples were only apples if they were green! Again, it wasn't the whole invisible meaning that counted, it was the visible detail.

Now, after many years, he understands the meaning of the word, but his attention to detail remains and in an unusual way. When I return from a lecture in Sweden or Finland and bring him a small apple-shaped gift (he has different evaluation criteria than we do), he is very happy with it. He now owns, for example, a Finnish apple (for us, it's a Cox) and a Swedish apple (Golden Delicious). We have to remember not to give him a red apple, because his immediate reaction is, "Is it poisoned?" Remember that the apple Snow White's angry stepmother gave her was red!

Thomas has many names for a bicycle. He has a 'bicycle', a 'tracto'r, a 'wheels in mud', a 'wheels on grass' and a 'small feet on pedals'. Many people think he is clever, but I know it's because he couldn't do otherwise. When I said, "Let's go for a bicycle ride," he didn't understand, because at that time he could see only his small feet on pedals. For him, the word 'bicycle' didn't yet have a general meaning.

A BICYCLE A WHEELS IN MUD

A TRACTOR

A WHEELS ON GRASS A SMALL FEET ON PEDALS

It must be extremely difficult to willingly call all sorts of different objects bicycle. On the other hand, if you look at a bicycle and see it as lots of different parts, it makes sense that the 'wheels on grass' is not the same as bicycle; the details are completely different from 'the wheels in mud' or 'the tractor' or 'the small feet on pedals'. Each kind of bicycle is different from the other.

A person with autism may not refer to all glasses as 'a glass' because each one looks different. For someone with detail perception, it is a lot to ask. Thomas calls glasses 'the furthest', 'a milkshake', 'a bomaglass', or 'a daily special'. To understand the differences, you have to have lived with him. Thomas calls one glass 'the furthest' because one day he wanted a drink. I took a glass out of the cupboard but it was not the one he wanted to drink from. I showed him a few other glasses in the cupboard. When I was on my tiptoes, barely able to reach a specific glass at the back of the shelf with my fingertips, I could see by his reaction that it was the one he wanted. I said, "Well, you want the furthest." Since then, 'the furthest' has been its name.

From his hyper-selective and perfectionist point of view, Thomas is right. How can glasses that look so different all be called by the same name?

The next glass is called 'the daily special'. His favourite TV show is F.C. De Kampioenen (The Champions). When one of the characters, Xavier, walks into the snack bar, he says, "I'll have the daily special." The the bartender returns with his glass of beer and says, "Here's your daily special."

Another character is called Boma and he is always drinking a 'Devil' (a special brand of beer) and thus the glass with Devil is called 'a bomaglass'. That kind of glass is also sometimes called 'my brand' and you can probably understand why.

He understands things the way he can, instead of understanding them the way we would like him to. A child with autism then tests his theories. Is this the way the world is put together? When I once said to Thomas, "Go sit on the chair," he didn't react at all. If you do not understand 'thinking through details', you might interpret his reaction as unwillingness. Often, we have to put up with reactions like, "He acts as if he can't hear," or "He understood alright, he just doesn't want to…" Yet, when you look at different kinds of chairs and the different details of each one, knowing what you do of hyper-selectivity, you try to put yourself in the shoes of a person with autism. If you found yourself in front of a chair such as the one that's circled, would you understand what I meant by, "Go sit on the chair"? Yes or no? Of course, you wouldn't.

Is he really a 'naughty boy' or is it in fact a question of what he has understood? The proof? When I said to Thomas, "Go sit on a stool," he did so immediately.

The word 'chat': Its origin and the solution to a riddle

When I bring Thomas to a new classroom for the first time, I make him understand that he'll have to stay with the new teacher by himself by saying, "Mum is going to chat." I know he understands that I am leaving without him. Here is why.

When I was going from specialist to specialist to find out what was wrong with him, Thomas was a very difficult little fellow. At one such meeting, a child psychiatrist couldn't answer any of my questions because while we spoke, Thomas was busy taking soil from a plant, switching the light on and off, opening and slamming the door, throwing the telephone on the floor, climbing onto the window sill, emptying the doctor's briefcase and so forth.

An assistant came to the rescue: she suggested taking Thomas to another room. She assured me that she would take good care of him. Thomas did not want to leave me and clung to my dress. So the assistant said, "Come with me, Thomas, your Mum has to chat some more." Chat was a new word for Thomas and he associated it with 'I can't stay with Mum'.

I still use the word in difficult situations. If, for instance, I want to go shopping with his sister and Thomas wants to come too, I first try explaining why he can't come with us. It doesn't work. Then, I remember the magic word, "Mum has to go chat," and it works. A therapist told me, "These are children with a user's guide." Indeed, I believe that this is often the case and that we should get to know the 'user's guide' of each person with autism.

Delayed Echolalia

> *"'Delayed Echolalia' means to speak with a certain delay, to repeat words literally. Many forms of echolalia could be considered an expression of hyper-selectivity. Echolalia is the typical language of a person who has a literal memory, good articulation and a less developed sense of 'meaning'."*

> Schuler & Prizant (1986)

In ordinary children, this phenomenon occurs between the ages of 18 and 36 months. For people with autism, it often occurs in association with higher developmental levels. Echolalic expressions are an attempt to survive in a difficult world; you use the language you understand instead of the language others want you to use. The words and sentences chosen often have a hyper-selective meaning: a detail will prevail because the speaker does not understand the greater meaning.

Think about the example of the glasses (the furthest, the daily special, my brand), and the word 'chat'. In the following example, Thomas doesn't understand the word 'beautiful'.

One day I was getting ready to go shopping. Thomas hears his brother Jeroen say, "Oh Mummy, where are you going, you look so beautiful!"

A few days later, I wear exactly the same clothes and Thomas repeats what his brother said, with the same intonation. "Where are you going, you look so beautiful?" To verify what I suspect, a few days later I put on the same clothes, but with other small boots. This time, Thomas doesn't say a thing. Beautiful for him means something quite concrete: little black boots with a red skirt, red blouse, a necklace, earrings and my hair up in a ponytail. All at once.

A similar communication difficulty: you try to understand as well as you can

When Joost started a new term at school, for some reason he no longer wanted to sit on his regular seat, although previously he had agreed to sit there. So his Mum was called upon. As soon as she saw the chair, she understood the problem. The chair was orange. One day Joost had cut his finger with a pair of orange scissors. Since then, for Joost, the colour orange was associated with pain. And so we see again that each child with autism has his own 'user's guide'.

About language and the dialect of objects

Back in the days when Thomas understood so little about the world, when everything seemed chaotic, when he didn't understand verbal requests and his tantrums went on and on all day long, I created tricks to explain things, without using words. As I observed him, I noticed that he grew more and more weary of all the talking. In work jargon, we call these tricks 'visual cues', but I have noticed that many mothers use this visual approach intuitively with their children, without giving it that name.

For example, to explain that we'd be leaving by car, I would show him the car keys. Showing him a plate meant that it was dinnertime. When we were to go shopping, I would show him a shopping bag. Thomas began to understand that he could come with me to the butcher's and the baker's when I showed him the shopping bag. It was like discovering the language of things for him.

Slowly, his feeling of panic disappeared. Imagine you have a very limited understanding of language and you never know where you are going when your Mum puts your coat on you! Everything became so much simpler for him. The better he understood the language of things, the less panicked he felt.

One day, his dad wanted to take him shopping. I reassured him. All you have to do, I said, is to show him the shopping bag and he'll understand where you are going with him. One hour later, Rutger returned home carrying Thomas under his arm. Thomas was screaming with all his might. The outing had been a disaster. Thomas had screamed, rolled over on the floor and displayed the full range of possible behaviour problems.

I could not understand what had happened. So I asked Rutger which bag he had taken. He showed it to me: it was the white bag, nothing like the shopping bag. Rutger had taken the bag we always use when we go to the swimming pool. Thomas, who was finally beginning to understand a bit of this complex world, felt betrayed. His father, by showing him the white bag, had told him they were going swimming and instead they went towards the butcher's! It was a breach of faith and he had protested in the only way he knew how.

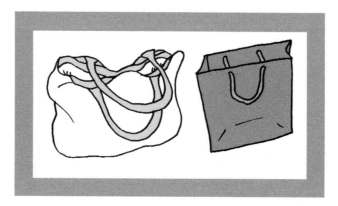

As far as the thought pattern of a person with autism goes, we can say that the language of objects contains many dialects. A word like glass can be called tumbler, goblet or wineglass. It can also be represented in different ways (a photograph, a drawing).

Objects also come in different shapes. A shopping bag is different from a swimming pool bag. Think of the many different shapes of everyday objects like toothbrushes or shampoos, for a start. Thomas and other children like him at certain ages can become upset if they are asked to brush their teeth with a short yellow toothbrush rather than the long red one they are used to.

Let's say you know shampoo comes in a container with a very specific shape and colour. And now there is another tiny container in our bathroom and daddy says it is shampoo too. It's a lie! How is one supposed to make sense of answers, rules, order and reliability? How do you deal with all the misunderstandings if you have autism? With the help of people around you, of course, but it is not an easy job for any of us.

A resistance to change, yes. But why? Many people with autism have difficulty with categorisation. They see the details, not the whole concept and so it is possible for a person with autism with a low developmental age to learn to go to lunch when he is given a plate, or to get coffee when he is given a cup. But what happens if someone else replaces his teacher and the new teacher gives him a different plate or another cup? A fit of anger? Aggressive behaviour? Resistance to change. Had the person with autism developed too close a relationship with the previous teacher? Was he too dependent on one specific person? These are possible interpretations. Or is it that he simply could not classify these different objects (plates of different shapes, textures and colours) as being part of the same group, 'plate', and therefore could not understand that they all have the same purpose and use?

> "Categorisation is a mental process that allows individuals to integrate new information with previous experience. This process does not usually occur through the memorisation of specific rules, but rather it typically involves an abstraction of information during learning. Without this ability, individuals would be overwhelmed by the complexity of their environment, being unable to make interferences based on past experience."

> Klinger & Dawson (1995)

A teenager with autism, who reads and writes, was continually asking the names of things. He held a glass in his hand, for example, asked the name of the 'thing' he was holding and then repeated, 'glass'. He then went on and asked for the word for a chair, a bottle, another bottle, another glass and so forth. He could not say the names of the various glasses, chairs and bottles by himself.

Now we stick labels with names on as many things as possible in his vicinity and he is happy. He reads the names of the objects and notices much more easily that many things of different shapes, sizes and colours share the same name like chair, glass and bottle. The world has become a little less confusing for him.

Another example: Thomas' reaction to a picture

Thomas is now nearly eleven; he can write and count. His sister Liesbeth is preparing him for a visit to the zoo. She lets him see all the pictures of the animals and teaches him their names. And then she goes over them again. Very good. Thomas knows the name for elephant, but to Liesbeth's surprise, he calls the hippopotamus an elephant and the rhinoceros as well. The elephants, hippos and rhinos may differ in shape and size, but in his own way, Thomas chose the colour of the hide (a visual detail) to learn the concept of 'elephant'.

Here's another more striking example. For us it may seem surrealistic, although Thomas' thinking is hyper-realistic. Thomas learnt the word giraffe and ever since has called a leopard 'giraffe' too even though the animal in the picture is lying on top of a tree, it has a much shorter neck, much smaller legs and a completely different head. You see, the detail he focused on to learn the concept of 'giraffe' was the pattern of the hide. One can see that the pattern on the leopard's fur is the same as the giraffe's. On the other side you can see the reproduction of a giraffe (same long neck, long legs…see illustration below in close-up) with a different skin pattern. For Thomas, this is not a giraffe.

Bizarrely, ordinary children don't notice the pattern as quickly. They immediately see what's more important. People with autism have a real problem in assigning meaning. They make an insufficient instinctive distinction between the trivial and the essential. In fact, it goes even further than that: look at the picture of the horse and the zebra on page 32. I remember my own brother describing the zebra as a horse in pajamas, or a horse dressed like a prisoner. The important thing is that an ordinary child will instinctively recognise the horseness of the zebra, a sort of horse-prototype, except that the zebra has pajamas on. You can also see the influence of imagination in the ordinary child's description.

If you look at the picture of the horse, put all the details together and you learn that this is called a horse, it does not mean that you will inevitably call the zebra a horse. You have to organise the information about the horse; you have to generalise about certain details to reach the essential, to end up with a kind of prototype or concept of 'horse' in your mind.

> "...Prototypes are formed after experience with a number of examples of a concept and there is some type of AVERAGING PROCESS which results in a prototype being formed."

Rosch (1973)

Temple Grandin notes that she does not have a general concept of 'dog'. When she thinks of 'dog', she thinks of specific dogs she has seen before.

> "Many people see a generalised generic church rather than specific churches and steeples when they read or hear the word 'steeple'. Their thought patterns move from a general concept to specific examples.
>
> My thinking pattern always starts with specifics and works towards generalisation in an associational and non-sequential way.
>
> Unlike those of most people, my thoughts move from video-like specific images to generalisation and concepts.
>
> For example, my concept of dogs is inextricably linked to every dog

I have ever known. It's as if I have a card catalogue of dogs I have seen, complete with pictures, which continually grows as I add more examples to my video library.

People with autism are not logical thinkers but associative thinkers."

Temple Grandin (1995)

Boys and Girls

At the time when it was still difficult for Thomas to recognise the difference between a boy and a girl, Thomas came home from school one day and said, "Mummy, Mieke is a girl!"

"Very good, Thomas! How do you know?"

The teacher said, "Mieke, you are a fine girl."

He found out whether Leen was a boy or a girl in his own way. The children were listening to a tale about Martin and Matilda. After hearing the story, the children had to act it out. The boys played Martin and the girls Matilda. Thomas observed attentively and noticed that little Leen was going to play the part of Matilda. Thus, he knew she was a girl.

When you see all the differences between male and female and notice that there are so many kinds of boys and girls, it's not easy to find the appropriate word to use. What detail must you select to know whether you should call someone lady, woman, man, girl or boy? In the supermarket, waiting in line at the cashier's, Thomas showed me a very old lady and said out loud, "Mummy, I think it's the girl's turn now!"

Confusion about the person or the right word?

Thomas came to a seminar with me. I had to wear a badge. Thomas was seven then and asked me what was written on it.

"Hilde De Clercq," I said.

Thomas asked, "What does that mean?"

"It's my name. I am Hilde de Clercq."

33

"So why do you say you're Mum?"

Two years later, I visit Thomas' class and the teacher introduces me. "Well children, Thomas' mother is here, what do you say?" The children and Thomas too say, "Good morning, ma'am!" I tell the children that I'm Hilde and that they can call me so. Some children do and Thomas says, "Hello, Hilde." I tell him that he should call me Mummy. He finds this quite complicated. "First you say you are Mummy then you say you are Hilde and now you're Mummy again!"

In the introduction, it was mentioned that we would first look at easy words, like table, giraffe, bicycle, etc: words for things and animals that are concrete, visible, that can be touched. But there are also many difficult words, such as young/old, fat/skinny and happy/sad. These words do not have an absolute meaning. The meaning varies according to the context. The previous example was already an illustration. An old lady is a girl, but in certain situations you wouldn't call her so. When is a girl old?

It's from a visible detail that Thomas will try to understand such words. When you show him an old lady, he'll remember a specific detail: she has a cane. It is not an old lady; it is a girl with a cane! And then it becomes an old lady. A lady can only be old if she has a cane.

One must nearly always broaden the word dictionary for each separate word.

> "Further, my mind constantly revises general concepts as I add new information to my memory library; it's like getting a new version of software for the computer..."

> Temple Grandin (1995)

Being old

Being old means having gray hair and wrinkles. You can also see age on the legs (Thomas calls them 'broken'), and old people die. So when he meets an old woman, he has to check all the signs of age. You can see how complicated this can get. What do you do when an old woman has wrinkles, 'broken' legs, but whose hair is not gray but black? Is she really old? In this case, Thomas' theory for understanding the world is being tested.

At the hospital, when we were visiting his great-grandmother, he said, "Your hair is gray, you have wrinkles, your legs are broken. You should have been dead a long time ago."

So grandmother is old and Mummy is young. But Mum's much older than he is. In fact she is old, but compared to grandma she is young. He tries to bring together the notions of young and old through a visual detail (in this case, his grandmother). Then one day he asked for some grandmother cheese. At first I thought he wanted some cheese he had had at his grandmother's, but in fact he simply meant 'old (mature) cheese'.

Big and small

A baby is small, but how difficult it becomes when someone says, "What a beautiful big baby you have."

Short and long

One day Thomas says in class, "My Mum does not have long hair."

But I do. We discuss the point and he holds to his statement. There must be something behind it.

Shortly thereafter, as I am about to cut his hair, he says:

"Mum, why must I have my hair cut?"

"Because it is too long."

"Do you have to get your hair cut too?"

"No, I don't."

So logically, my hair is not long. Notice that he does not say 'short', but 'not long'. He is such a perfectionist, so careful and so afraid of being wrong. He tries so hard to do his best.

Chapter 2

Thinking through Details:
Emotions and Social Behaviour

*"...This cognitive pathology seems to consist largely of an inability
to reduce information through the appropriate extraction of crucial
features such as rules and redundancies. The impairment in these
processes imposes well-remembered, stereotypical and restricted
behaviour patterns, which become increasingly inappropriate as the
requirements for complex, flexible codes increase. It is in the areas
of language development and social interaction, which are governed
by such complex rules, that the autistic child's cognitive impairment
becomes most evident..."*

Hermelin (1978)

If people with autism have difficulty getting beyond the superfluous to
reach the essential and if as a result they cling to details in a
desperate attempt to get a grasp on life, then obviously the world of
emotions must be even harder for them. How are you going to
comprehend an inner emotion if you are holding on tight to a detail,
which may have nothing to do with it?

The 'autism-dictionary'

1. Happy and sad

For us, the difference is obvious. A mouth
curved up means happy, a mouth curved
down means sad. We recognise this easily,
because we have an 'abstract idea' of
what happy is and what sad is, so that
even without seeing a specific expression
of joy or sorrow, we still recognise that it
belongs to the same 'pattern'.

For people with autism, who tend to understand things literally and to cling to specific external details, it is not so easy. In other words, seen from their perspective it seems strange that the one curve means happiness because you must admit, you've never met anyone with exactly that kind of curve for a smile, or with the one for sadness. And we haven't mentioned identifying more complex feelings such as jealousy, feeling betrayed, etc.

Thomas fixes on an external detail in order to understand an inner meaning. When I heard him crying in his bed one day and asked, "Why are you crying, are you sad?" he replied, "His pillow is wet." Now, a few years later, he can express himself directly, without going through an external detail (although he had gone through an echolalic period and was using the word 'sad' without really understanding it).

Well, as parents you try your best. We taught them to sort pictures – this one is sad, this one is happy, this one is angry and it worked. Thomas put all the sad faces together and all the happy ones too. So he could do it!

Then one day, when his sister was getting very angry with him, he went and stood in front of her and asked, seemingly a bit lost, "Liesbeth, all those lines on your face, what are they for?"

As an exercise, another little boy had to select happy faces and sad faces. He made only one mistake: he put a happy face together with the sad faces. When asked why, he replied, "In the happy faces, you can see the teeth; you don't see them here, right?"

Once again, this example shows that a person with autism may tend to focus on a single visual detail. But for him the important thing is,

which detail should he select? From the
point of view of a person with autism,
there are no absolute rules. You can be
sad and be in tears, but you can also be
sad and be tearless. You can have tears in
your eyes because you are sad, but you
also have tears in your eyes because you
are happy or moved! And what about
more subtle emotions, like being
embarrassed, moved, touched, nervous
or feeling huffy?

Above all, faces are not static and you can't do a close-up on the
expression of a particular emotion, you can't freeze it and hold on to it
for a while. When we think of all the many different steps Van Dalen
(1994) needs to process the word 'hammer' (and in that case it was a
static object), we can understand how complicated it is to read an
emotion: it is non-static, different in each person and can disappear or
change immediately.

Normally gifted people with autism have made us aware that we use
various sensory channels at the same time (touch, sound and sight for
example) to process information. For us it all happens at the same
time, automatically. But for them it happens in 'mono': listening is
easier if you don't need to actively look at the same time, looking is
improved if you don't have to actively listen at the same time.

How can you tell that Daddy Dalmatian and Mummy Dalmatian are
happy and proud, that one puppy is tired and another one bored, if
you don't have an inner picture of what happiness, pride and
boredom are?

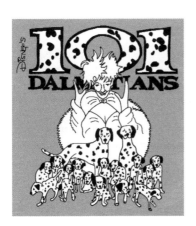

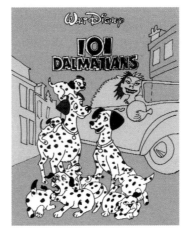

For Thomas there is an additional complication: a dog can't really be a daddy or a Mummy. Daddy is daddy and Mummy is Mummy, right?

2. Love and marriage

When Joke, Thomas's girl cousin, was looking at a video of Cinderella, all was quiet in the room. At the end of the film you could tell by the music what would happen next. Cinderella was dancing with the prince, they looked very much in love and sighing with excitement and relief Joke said, "They are going to get married." Ever since, Thomas has been asking people he meets, "Are you married?" If they answer yes, he continues, "So, you turned around?" If they say, "No," he then says, "So you did not turn around?"

People are a bit confused about what to think? For Thomas, it's very clear: he saw Cinderella and the prince dancing ('turning around'), he heard his cousin say, "Get married," and so the association is made. The meaning behind the pictures, the faces, the music and the words 'get married' were completely unnoticed by him.

At the dinner table, Thomas always sits next to me. I look lovingly at him and wink. Then I ask him; "What does it mean when Mummy looks at you this way?"

"Sardines," he answers.

In The Aristocats, the street cat in love says to the lady cat, "Your eyes are like sardines," so the lady cat winks with her beautiful eyes. Thank goodness his sister Liesbeth understands the association!

Thomas has seen the video of The Lady and the Tramp one thousand times at least, but recently Joke noticed that the two were eating a piece of spaghetti together. "They're in love, maybe they'll get married." It's getting more complicated. Getting married now seems to mean sharing spaghetti as well.

Just when he thought he knew the meaning of getting married, i.e., dancing together round and round he sees another video with two cats on a roof, their tails intertwined. Jasper, Thomas's cousin, looks at the video and comments sweetly, "Oh, they're going to get married."

So Thomas files a new picture in his card catalogue: getting married is dancing together round and round, entangling tails, chewing on the same piece of spaghetti. But sardines can also lead to marriage...

One day, I was feeling very proud for it seemed that Thomas had finally cracked the meaning of the word 'marriage'. He opened a little book and showed me the Dalmatians. "See, Mum, they are getting married."

"Good, Thomas, very good. How do you know that?"

He looks at the text. "Look, Mum, it's written here, 'They're getting married'."

3. To be frightened, to be teased and making fun of someone

We try to make Thomas understand the meaning of the word 'surprised'. We practice in front of the mirror. Thomas is surprised – he makes a sound and puts his hand on his heart. We repeat the word surprised. He seems to have understood. And now, a little story will illustrate the point.

Once in a while Thomas makes the coffee. He is very proud of this. Sometimes on a weekend I will tell him that he can prepare the morning coffee and that I'll get up and be surprised at the sight of the coffee he has made for me. And so it happens exactly like that. I get up and after seeing the coffee, I make the expected sound, put my hand on my heart and Thomas is very happy to see me surprised.

Once, while I was on a training course in Sweden, I received a phone call. Thomas was being unbelievably difficult again. His brothers tried to please him. They had promised to be surprised as soon as he had finished his game. He was asking them to be surprised non-stop all day long. Even if they had been surprised a hundred times per day he would persist, telling them to do it over and over again. Once I was back, I immediately saw what was wrong. They weren't surprised the way he had learned. A single detail was missing: although they made the right shriek, they didn't bring their hands to their hearts. I sorted it out by asking the children to shriek and also put their hands on their hearts. Then it was OK.

Once, Thomas talked about letters being scared. Psychotic use of the language? People around him grew worried; this talk reminded them of the poisoned apple episode. But I knew that for Thomas you don't need to look for symbolic explanations. The answer will be found instead in his concrete, down to earth, over-selective thinking. Which numbers were scared? 0 and 6 (see the drawing on page 42), and number 8 is a doubly frightened number.

They are making fun of me...

Thomas is more and more conscious that he has difficulty understanding certain things. He often has the impression that people are making fun of him and unfortunately, it is sometimes true. This makes him very angry.

At the dinner table one evening, he suddenly feels his sister is making fun of him. I ask him why he thinks this, since his sister loves him so much! He explains why:

- ◆ I sit down at the table
- ◆ so does my sister
- ◆ she is sitting across from me
- ◆ she looks at me
- ◆ her mouth looks like this
- ◆ her eyes are like that

- there are lines under her eyes

- she does, "Hihihihi"

- so she must be making fun of me.

Notice the huge difficulty he has in understanding the concept 'making fun of'. He describes all the details that together mean 'making fun of'. Read again how Van Dalen (1994) builds up his hammer-concept.

How should he react when he is being teased? It happens often during recess and he is defenceless. Chris, the speech therapist, is going to help him. She starts by drawing him a picture of the whole situation. Thomas perfectly understands these kinds of drawings. If he gets teased again, he'll have to show that he is angry. But how do you show anger?

They practice a lot and here is what happens: he's at break and the kids tease him. He runs into the speech therapist's office, looks for a mirror, tries to make the same facial expression that he has been taught (this is how to look angry), then runs back all the while trying to maintain the same facial expression in order to show his angry face to the other children. You can imagine how the children react to this.

Unfortunately, there is more. One day I noticed that his legs were all bruised. With a lot of patience I managed to get him to tell me, painfully, that some children had kicked him. I told him that this was called 'bullying' (teasing) and that he should go and tell the teacher if it happened again.

A few days later, I found out through indirect questioning that some children pulled on his woollen cap. I reminded him that he was to go to the teacher when that happened. "But that is only if I am being bullied!" he argued. "That's bullying, too," I reply. "But isn't being bullied when they kick me?"

From that day on, I began to make small dictionaries for Thomas, word catalogues in fact.

Being bullied is when:

- they kick me

- they pull on my cap

- they pull on my coat

- they hit me

- ◆ they scratch me
- ◆ they insult me.

Insulting me is:

- ◆ if they say I'm dumb
- ◆ if they say I'm stupid
- ◆ if they say I'm a moron
- ◆ if they say naughty words to me.

Understanding emotions and social situations is far more complicated than sorting out fruits and vegetables. Is harassing also pulling on trousers? Or is that being insulted? Or impolite?

Being impolite is:

- ◆ swearing
- ◆ shouting
- ◆ speaking with your mouth full
- ◆ taking other children's food
- ◆ yelling at Mum
- ◆ yelling at the teacher.

The list seems endless. Is it also impolite to yell at dad? To yell at a friend? And what about if it's someone who's just hurt you? If someone yells an insult, is it being impolite or insulting? So, when a child yells at him, he says, "You are im-po-lite." This is how the word has been taught to him: he mimics the voice and intonation of the person who taught him these words. Thomas has been saying it that way over and over for months. And each detail is important: the pronunciation, the stress on the syllables. This is how we see that repeating words can also be linked to 'thinking through details' and having difficulties with global meanings.

> "For a long time, you understand so little of a language and it requires such an effort, that you begin to believe that you also have to imitate the voice of the person who is saying the words. You don't seem to be aware of the fact that these words can be pronounced in different ways, and that you can use other words to say the same thing."

Therese Joliffe (1992)

So when the teacher gets angry with Thomas because he hasn't been good, you can imagine what happens. Thomas reacts by saying that the teacher had been im-po-lite to him.

In a department store, a cashier calls a colleague for a price-check. She is doing this with a very hard voice. Thomas says out loud, "They are im-po-lite."

The painting, The Cheaters by Georges de la Tour, is very well known in the world of autism. Uta Frith used it to explain the difficulties people with autism have with the development of a Theory of Mind.

A Theory of Mind is the skill people need to understand and to interpret the inner states of mind of others, i.e. feelings, ideas, thoughts and intentions...

Having developed a Theory of Mind implies that one is able to predict and to take into account inner states of people.

After having explained 'thinking through details' we shouldn't find it surprising that people with autism have trouble dealing with social situations. Which surface detail can be used to understand a complex social situation? Social interaction is defined as 'abstract symbols in permanent movement'. For a person with autism, processing and understanding complex social situations is extremely challenging. Even Temple Grandin says she feels like 'an anthropologist from Mars' when confronted with many people in social situations.

Let's look at an illustration of the painting

First, we see the expressive eyes of the ladies in the centre. They are cheating. But how do we explain this to a person with autism? Through what detail in the eyes can you tell they're cheating? It's easier to show Thomas the card hidden behind the player's back. But then Thomas thinks that cheating is hiding cards behind one's back – it's easy to understand the association.

So cheating becomes hiding cards behind one's back. We'll have to go back to our card catalogue and add an entry under the word 'betrayal'. This is how we can help him. And yet, we cannot fully help him because there are so many ways to betray someone and we can't foresee every possibility. He remains vulnerable. Even Temple Grandin says that although she can read people's basic feelings, she can't understand subtle signs of betrayal; she is lost in front of them. If we understood the huge problem people with autism face making sense of social behaviour, we would not find it so surprising that many people with autism have an echo-like imitation behaviour.

Lorna Wing (1976) describes them as 'active but odd' (probably a synonym for social 'echo-behaviour'). These 'active but odd' people want to be just like us, but don't understand the subtle rules of social behaviour and so imitate social behaviour down to its minute details as a survival strategy. Like echolalia, echo-behaviour is quite misleading.

> "You learn to ape human behaviour," her husband interpolated. "I still don't understand what's behind the social conventions. You observe the front, but..."

Oliver Sacks (1995)

> "I tried imitating other people. Now that I was with people more, I had to be someone. People asked me what I wanted, what I thought. I took features from people I met and added them to me. I often took features from people who seemed very self-confident. I did this immensely skillfully. I became a chameleon – if I adopted Karin's way of sighing as she spoke, I could use it with everyone except Karin and if I adopted Maria's taste in music, then I didn't talk about music with Maria. I was an empty jar that could be filled with anything."

Gunilla Gerland (1998)

"Children, she feels, are already far advanced by the age of three or four, along a path that she, as an autistic person, has never advanced far on. Little children, she feels, already 'understand' other human beings in a way she can never hope to do."

Temple Grandin in Sacks (1995)

"I asked her about the Greek myths. She said that she had read many of them as a child, and that she thought of Icarus in particular – how he had flown too near the sun and his wings had melted and he had plummeted to his death…But the loves of the gods, I ascertained, left her unmoved- and puzzled. It was similar with Shakespeare's plays. She was bewildered, she said, by Romeo and Juliet ("I never knew what they were up to")…

She said that she could understand 'simple, strong, universal' emotions but was stumped by more complex emotions and the games people play; "Much of the time," she said, "I feel like an anthropologist on Mars."

Oliver Sacks (1995)

Chapter 3

The 'Other' Imagination

It takes a huge effort for people with autism just to understand daily life! It requires great intellectual exertion for them even to understand that a green toothbrush and a red toothbrush are both toothbrushes.

Five things that we ride, each one different from the other, are all called a 'bicycle'. Twelve things, from which we drink, each different in shape and colour, all have the same name – glass.

And then we have toys. Little cars, small trains, teddy bears, so far from reality (which is difficult enough in itself) and with so many details.

One of the most important questions parents ask is, "Why doesn't he play?" Let's try to see things through the eyes of a child with autism. His thinking is literal so it is very difficult for him to understand symbols. On different separate levels, spoken language, written language, pictures and objects are all symbols, which means they take the place of something else. The word 'horse', for example, replaces the real animal. For a child with autism, reality is very difficult to understand and reality is hidden in all these symbols.

Ordinary people, the surrealists, like to play with reality. They pretend to phone, they pretend a doll is a human being, they pretend a child's toy train is a real train. Turning reality upside down is lots of fun for the surrealist, but a real nightmare for a hyper-realist.

Ian, a boy with autism, knows each and every brand of car, but he doesn't understand why a VW, a Ford and a Honda are all called cars. Two red cars can be different brands, colours and the size may vary. What is one to make of these pictures of cars?

Thomas recognises the car on the top, but not the one on the bottom, which is made of Lego. If you give him instructions to build a model car, he will be able to construct it in no time and do it correctly. But he wouldn't call his construction a car. That's taking reality too far.

In the literature on autism, one learns that there are iconic and non-iconic gestures. Pointing is iconic, which means there is a visual similarity between the gesture and the meaning. The connection is obvious.

Comforting a child by stroking his head is non-iconic, because there is no obvious link between the action and its meaning. You need to go beyond a literal perception. This gesture is too vague. The meaning has to be thought out.

Some of the toy telephones also seem too 'open': the link to reality is hardly visible at all. That they really are telephones must be thought out; one must go beyond the external perception. They are not real telephones. A person with autism feels he has been made a fool of, somehow cheated.

What makes toys attractive to ordinary children? Things like colour, texture and design…These things are often extra difficulties and make them harder to understand for children with autism. This is why we finally gave up on most toys for Thomas. We wanted him to be able to recognise things, so we adapted ourselves to his perception. We started from his point of view, using his thought process.

> "When I was four, I wanted an accordion…I never wished for toys –
> I usually didn't know what they were for…I wanted real things, I
> didn't think of toys as proper birthday presents…

I opened all the presents lying on my bed, but there was no accordion. However, in one of the parcels was a hideous little object in blue plastic. This, they said, was an accordion. "Just what you wanted," they said. I was confused and dismayed. I didn't understand.

This could not be an accordion. This was something small, ugly and pale blue. I'd seen accordions, after all. They were beautiful, dark red and gleaming, with rows of white buttons. Shiny and with a lovely sound inside them. But they showed me that this thing was an accordion, that you could play on it. It said toot when you pulled it out and the same toot when you pushed it back. How could they say this was an accordion? It had none of the characteristics I associated with an accordion...So it was no accordion to me. This blue thing must be something quite different – anyone could see that. This thing was neither big, red nor shiny. It hadn't many buttons and it didn't sound nice. And yet they said it was an accordion – were they trying to deceive me?

It was something to do with language."

Gunilla Gerland (1998)

Take stuffed animals. There are all kinds: teddy bears, dogs, dolphins, whales, elephants, panthers. But there are no similarities between the real animal and the stuffed ones. Why do we suddenly call this bear a teddy bear? Okay, because it is small, made of fluff and we can cuddle it. But once we learn that a bear is a teddy bear, what about all the other animals that are also stuffed? If you compare a stuffed elephant and a dressed teddy bear, they hardly look alike.

One day, Thomas was allowed to bring a stuffed animal to school with him because the children were going to learn something about them. He said that the other children had brought different stuffed animals. When he got back home, he insisted that the stuffed animal he had taken to school was a stuffed animal, but the ones lined up on his bed weren't.

Of course, we could teach Thomas that all the animals belonged to the same stuffed animal group, but on his own he wouldn't grasp the relationship as normal children do. It requires a lot of effort on his part and causes quite a bit of grief. So you only accept such information from people you trust.

Liesbeth is nine and Thomas nearly seven.

"Come, Thomas, let's make a doll's house."

"Yes, let's make a doll's house."

Thomas goes and gets his pillow and his blanket – not for the dolls, but for himself. And while his sister is organising it all, he is already lying on the floor.

"So, let's see...The veranda is our house."

"Yes, our house."

"And the closet is the doll's bedroom."

"Yes, the closet is the bedroom."

"We'll get some shoeboxes; they'll sleep in them."

"Are they going to sleep in there? They are shoeboxes, you know!"

"Yes, but now they are little beds for the dolls."

"Yes. Little beds for the dolls."

"The tissues are the sheets and the towels will be the blankets."

Meanwhile, Thomas goes to the kitchen and takes a ladle out of the drawer. He goes back to his sister and says:

"And this ladle, this ludle...it's...our ladle."

Peeters (1997)

And we were so happy because he was playing!

Here we can see two monkeys; one is different from the other. For Thomas, the second monkey is a monkey, the first is a statue (and don't ask me why).

When we look at Duplo toys, we find a lot of different monkeys. How do we explain that we call the picture on the Duplo box a monkey? Why is a piece of duplo called a monkey? There is simply no explanation. In fact, you can recognise the nose, but how do we see that? Duplo is made for little children at an early developmental age and little children understand it. They aren't concerned with how closely it resembles a real monkey. Shape, colour, texture, everything is different. Yet for Thomas, with his perception and thought process, it is absolutely going against nature to call a Duplo thing a monkey. Not only that. It's hard enough for him to see it's a monkey. But then to be expected to play with it!

- ◆ Make believe the monkey is climbing a tree.
- ◆ Pretend he is climbing.
- ◆ Pretend there is a tree.
- ◆ As if it were a monkey.
- ◆ And then surely make believe that the monkey is a human being, right?
- ◆ Act like the monkey can speak like a human being?

Such a surrealist adventure....Forget it.

Thomas has practiced a lot of pretend play. Once my leg was in a cast and he pretended he had hurt his foot too. He walked with crutches around the house, echoing, "I'll surely be in pain using these for the next eight weeks." In the evening, I couldn't climb up to the top bunk to give him his goodnight kiss. I suggested kissing him at the foot of the bed and pretended to be on the little ladder. I put him on my lap and pretended to be climbing up the ladder with my fingers and said, "See, I'm on the ladder for your goodnight kiss." Thomas answered, seemingly worried, "But Mum, how are you going to get down?" And I thought that he really had understood this time.

We also try to keep fairy tales as realistic as possible. Remember Snow White and the poisoned red apple? What I do is tell stories to Thomas based on what he has he experienced, instead of introducing him to a fantasy world that he cannot understand.

In the video, The Jungle Book, Thomas noticed that the sky in the background grows lighter and lighter as the film progresses. But meanwhile, he didn't notice that Mowgli was about to be strangled by the snake. He did notice, however, that one vulture was darker than the others.

Thomas likes to play with a construction game. The bricks, windows and doors look like real ones, only much smaller (like miniature cars, as a matter of fact) and you don't have to use your imagination to play with it. The box says, "Little carpenters can build with real bricks, using child-friendly cement and high quality plastic windows and doors. You can supplement your basic kit with a variety of additional kits to plan and build your very own dream house according to your imagination." As you can imagine, Thomas always follows the instructions. Making a house according to his imagination is too much to ask of him.

Once he wanted to have a dwarf, but he wanted a 'real' dwarf. I felt moved. I was so happy that at last he had a wish like an ordinary child. When we went for a walk, he saw a small dwarf in a garden made of plastic or stone and said, "Look, Mum, that's a real dwarf, I want one just like it."

The following anecdote has already been quoted in the book, Autism, from theoretical understanding to educational intervention. But I feel that it is important to mention it here, because it's another story to add to the concept of surprise.

> "The holidays were coming up soon, with all the surprises that entailed. I really dislike this time of the year because Thomas' life is completely disturbed. But I discovered a way to make the best of it. A surprise should be pleasant, and for him pleasant means knowing what is going to happen in advance. So now I show him a catalogue with the gift Saint Nicholas will bring him and what he can do with it. We cut the picture out of the catalogue and glue it onto a piece of

red paper. Then I make a calendar using white paper, one sheet for each day until Christmas and lastly the red sheet. This way he can tear off a page each day and he'll know how much time is left till Christmas. We also go to the shop and look at the gift, because it always looks different in reality compared to the catalogue. If it's a game, we'll try to rent it from a game-rental service to be sure that the game is not too difficult for him and that he will be able to use it.

On Christmas Eve, I tell him where the surprise is hidden and in what sort of wrapping. His brothers and sister feel that a surprise is no fun if you know everything beforehand. But on the big day when he sees the red paper on his calendar, for the first time it truly is a happy moment for all the children, including Thomas. This time, he doesn't throw the toy, he does not holler. What he sees in front of him, is something he expected, it was planned. He knows what his surprise will be. He winks and then opens and closes his mouth at the same time. One of his little hands seems to have left his body and he uses the other to pull on a strand of hair. He jumps awkwardly twice and I burst into tears seeing him so happy."

Peeters (1994)

Thomas found this predictability very helpful, but there were other things that he picked up from this in his own hyper-selective way. One was that a surprise had to be wrapped in red paper and look exactly the same as the gift that he had received on that first real celebration. A luminous doll was wrapped in that package with the red wrapping paper. So this is what a gift looked like for Thomas. Other packages were simply not gifts.

So we practiced this at home. We slowly introduced other presents that were wrapped in different colour wrapping paper. Gifts could be different too, but he had to know that beforehand, or else it wouldn't be considered a surprise. For his birthday, he got a luminous doll. We practiced at school. Helen bought a present for her Mum and wrapped it up nicely. The children were curious. What had Helen bought for her Mum? What could be in the package? Thomas was certain that it would be a luminous doll. There is one more little detail to add. After he got his surprise, he wanted to be cuddled in my bed and so he unwrapped his gift there. Since then, all packages have to be opened in Mum's bed.

The power of hyper-selectivity and detail can be overwhelming because of this lack of simple insight. Red wrapping paper is the most important, but we also have to know what the surprise is going to be beforehand and gifts have to be opened in Mum's bed. Change the details and the order and you ruin the event in a miserable way.

"The constant change of things never seemed to give me any chance to prepare myself for them. Because of this, I found pleasure and comfort in doing the same things over and over again."

Donna Williams (1992)

"This over-selectivity has some major consequences. First of all, autistic persons have difficulties with familiarisations because everything always looks anew for them. In other words they feel little whatsoever to change something in their environment or they even don't want to change anything because, for them, variation exists in abundance.

This autistical striking characteristic trait, a resistance for change, is better known as 'insistence on sameness'."

Van Dalen (1995)

So you can see why some children with autism will take great interest in some tiny detail of a toy. They will spin the wheels of a car endlessly instead of driving it around and seeing it in its entirety, a whole object with a logical meaning.

Other children will try to play like normal children. Often, it may seem that they are playing games using symbols but if you look closely, you will notice that they always play the same game over and over again, in all its detail.

Thomas will give his doll a bath, for example. But it always has to be in the little red bathtub in a specific place in the garden. It is always the same doll and he always washes its hair (a doll without hair by the way!) with the same green shampoo. He always proceeds in exactly the same way: first, he smells the shampoo, then he pours it. He has very little empathy for the doll as, eyes wide open, it is then shoved in the tub. It is not real symbolic play, it is more like echo-play.

Hyper-selective thought also makes it necessary to remember each and every detail. If even one detail is changed, nothing works. Often, we hear that people with autism are anchored to routines. You might say that these routines stem from an over-selective understanding of specific actions connected to a specific location.

How often I dreamed that Thomas would learn to play like my other children, that he would come to understand that a doll stands for a little child, that he would really love a doll because it was like a child, that he would hug, stroke and kiss it too. It is only when you have a child for which all that is very difficult that you realise what a miracle it is to play a simple game. Sometimes, you feel so overcome with sadness, your whole life seems overwhelmed with sorrow. It makes it even harder if those around you don't understand and ask questions like, "And you even need to show him how to play!?" These feelings are expressed in the following poem. I have read it so often. And so often it has made me feel sad and angry, then sad some more and angry again. If you have a child with autism, you will recognise the feelings.

The Doll Theatre

The little girl was blonde.

So was the doll.

The little girl had brown eyes.

The doll's eyes were blue.

The little girl loved her doll dearly.

No-one knew if the doll loved the little girl.

But the little girl died.

The doll remains.

Now, no-one knows if the girl still loves the doll.

And the doll couldn't fit in a single drawer.

The doll opens all the trunks.

The doll breaks into all the closets.

The doll is bigger than everything in the house.

The doll is everywhere.

The doll fills up the house.

We have to get rid of the doll.

We have to make the doll disappear forever.

We must kill the doll. Bury it.

The Doll.
Carlos Queiroz (1966)

If playing, make believe and simple toys are too complicated for children with autism, it makes sense for them to stick to routines that can be repeated over and over. They will feel more comfortable setting up schedules, memorising facts and data or, like Thomas, remembering brands of cars. Such a world is less confusing because facts and data are more stable than people. You can count on facts. They don't change.

> *"Categorisation abilities provide individuals with an understanding of their environment and thereby produce in them feelings of control over their environments.*
>
> *If persons with autism have category impairments, they may engage in repetitive behaviours as a means of getting a sense of control."*

Rosch (1973)

Dinosaurs on bicycles? A dinosaur roller-skating? A dinosaur with a Walkman on his head? What is amusing to normal children can be stupid or even frightening for children with autism. Indeed, some elements can only belong to a specific context.

For a normal child, this could be considered pretty: a horse with flowers on its head. For people with autism, this kind of mistake is a disaster. They do their best to understand reality, putting all kinds of details together and in their thought process, some details only belong to a specific situation. Flowers are supposed to be in gardens, in fields, in the grass, but not on a head of a horse. For them, it is as absurd as finding a shoe on a plate or a pen in our soup. There are two sides to this kind of mistake: for some it can be a real calamity, for others it can be very amusing.

During a gross motor skills exercise, someone asked an adult woman with autism to carry marbles from one side of a field to the other. She was asked to carry one marble at a time in a ladle. When she saw the spoon in the middle of a sports activity, she began to cry. It can't be! The world is topsy-turvy. A ladle belongs in the kitchen. She understand little enough about the world she lived in as it was and her little bit of understanding, her tiny stronghold was being taken away.

Our children had made a snowman. Thomas did not agree. He took off the scarf and the hat and threw them back into the hallway near the coat rack. He put the two pieces of coal that had been used for the eyes next to the stove, and ate the carrot. Didn't these people know any better?

Sometimes though, Thomas found such mistakes amusing. He would laugh for hours and it was hard to get him to stop. To make him happy, we'd put a kitchen glass once in a while in the bathroom. When he would see it, he'd roll about with laughter. That glass does not belong there. What a funny surprise!

All these examples show us how very difficult it is for people with autism to deal with our fantasies, imagination, decoration and aesthetics. As if reality was not complicated enough, a reality in which everything and everyone has its place, its people, its activities and its details.

In Thomas's reality, everything does have a specific place, with certain people, activities and details in it. Behind his reality is our reality, a make-belief reality. He tries endlessly to travel and find his way between these two realities. We do the same, going from our reality to his and back. But the energy involved for him to do so is far greater than the energy we use to do this.

Unfortunately, autism is still all too often associated with the cliché of withdrawal into oneself. In fact, the word autism is rather inadequate to express the 'other' thought process. People with autism have similarities and could be better compared to people from a different cultural background.

> *"Being autistic does not mean being inhuman. But it does mean being alien. It means that what is normal for other people is not normal for me, and what is normal for me is not so for other people. In some ways, I am terribly ill-equipped to survive in this world, like an extraterrestrial stranded without an orientation manual. But my personhood is intact. My selfhood is undamaged. I find great value and meaning in my life and I have no wish to be cured of myself...*
>
> *Recognise that we are equally alien to each other, that my ways of being are not merely damaged versions of yours...*
>
> *Question your assumptions. Define your terms. Work with me to build bridges between us."*

Jim Sinclair (1992)

Part 2

Educational Help

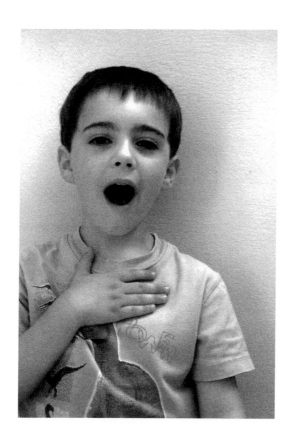

Chapter 4

Daily Timetables and 'Thinking through Details'

People with autism seem to be lost in time. For them, processing information is extremely difficult because by nature it is abstract, invisible and fugitive. Even more abstract, invisible and 'temporal' is time itself.

So, an important step towards becoming independent would be to learn how to anticipate the events of the day. This would give someone the feeling his life was under some control and would naturally make him happier.

A daily schedule or agenda, an 'autism' timetable, is always very individualised in form (using words, pictures or objects), in duration (how many activities are mentioned) and in use (does he take the symbols with him to the following activity or not). The topic, including all of the things mentioned above, has been covered in-depth in numerous publications. The intent of this chapter is to see how time processing may be influenced by thinking through detail.

Daily schedule with use of objects

A person with autism will be shown, by the use of concrete objects, the activities he will be carrying out that day. We pointed out earlier that in the language of objects there are dialects: a shopping bag is different from a swimming gear bag; a green glass looks different from a red glass.

If, for example, I am learning French and I learn that the word for glass is 'verre', I will be upset if someone then uses the word 'goblet'. For someone beginning to learn the language of objects, a green glass is as different from a red glass as the colours (a detail) are different. Let's say we want to explain to a child that we are going to wash his hair. The object we use is a bottle of shampoo. Each time we wash his hair we will use the same bottle until he understands the association: they show me the shampoo and it means that my hair is going to be washed. Some children will eventually understand that another type of shampoo can also be used for the same activity, but for others this is too big a leap.

Practically speaking, there are two possibilities here:

> Either the person learns categorisation, e.g. that all the different kinds of shampoos belong to the same category and therefore they will have the same function, (categories can be taught through sorting exercises, in this case by using real objects)...

> or it remains too difficult and we must keep on using the same object.

Objects on cards

Simon is a non-verbal boy with autism and has a relatively young developmental age. He loves Smarties. He has a card with a real Smartie glued onto it so that he can ask for some. The card is plasticised (otherwise he would immediately eat the candy and then not learn how to ask for Smarties).

One day, we placed a card next to Simon's plate, but this time, to my astonishment, he didn't ask for a Smartie. When I took a close look at the communication card, I suddenly noticed that I had glued an M&M on it instead of a Smartie. For Simon, the difference was huge.

When we want to tell Jan that it's time to wash, he is given a card on which a washcloth is glued. For some residents, we always have to use the same glove or cloth. For others, it makes no difference which one we use.

Schedule with pictures

For many people with autism, photos are more iconic. They express meaning more clearly than drawings. But not for all, because on some photos there is far too much information.

Herman is a teenager with autism. His father was going to pick him up at school. The teacher placed a photograph of his father on his schedule. She noticed that Herman was excited and went back and forth regularly to look at the picture. When his father came to collect him, the teacher mentioned this to Herman's dad, who was happy his son was looking forward to his arrival. However, in the car Herman was tense and his dad couldn't understand why. It all ended in a tantrum. Later, Herman's parents figured out what Herman was thinking. On the picture that the teacher showed him, one can see a chair in the background that is at their country house. So Herman thought that that was where his father was taking him. Yet when his dad picked him up, they went the wrong way. For Herman, this was the cause of the huge misunderstanding.

This example shows you the problem with photos on a timetable. They often contain too much information and some children with autism will focus on a detail that for them has a very specific meaning. This can lead to stressful situations.

Suppose you think your child knows that it is time to eat each time you show him the photo of the kitchen. From the photo, he thinks he is going to get cornflakes (aren't they in the photo) but he gets a sandwich instead. Or it could be the other way around. He doesn't like cornflakes and in the photo there is a box of the hated cornflakes.

Having things tailor-made is essential in the choice of an appropriate schedule. It is essential to individualise not only according to the level of the child's understanding (the level of abstraction), which is crucial, but also according to his level of hyper-selectivity, that is, the way he processes visual information.

A photo of a plate means more to Eric than the picture of a dining room, because the former gives him the information he needs. When he sees the photo of a plate, he knows immediately that he can go eat. It's completely different for Frank. If you give him a photo of a plate, he'll go to the dining room looking for a plate of the same size, colour or design and of course, this is not what the teacher wants to communicate to him. On the other hand, when he sees a picture of the dining room, it's very clear to him that he has to go there and eat.

When I began a daily schedule with Thomas, I knew for sure that he understood photos and it thus seemed the obvious choice for his schedule. Soon it became obvious that many of them were unusable. Thomas would remember every detail of each picture. If Thomas saw the picture of the bicycle, he understood perfectly well that he could go cycling, but he wanted to wear the exact same clothes and shoes as in the photograph. I remember that we were having the house completely refurbished at the time. Nothing was in its proper place, doors, floors and so on. It was already difficult enough for Thomas, but when we had these communication problems with the photos it became even more chaotic. From his point of view, it was quite strange. You do your best so that everything looks exactly like in the picture and that's still not good enough.

We had a similar situation with the bathroom. Thomas understood that he had to use the bathroom, but in his perfectionist way, he wanted everything to be exactly as it was in the picture – the little bottle of shampoo on the left, the big green one in the middle, the conditioner on the right, the talcum powder box here and the dirty towel hanging on the wall.

When Thomas went to a class for children with autism, the teacher had given him a picture of a blue bus with a child climbing onto it and had said, "Look, this is little Tommy in the morning. The bus will come by and pick you up to go to school." The next morning, a little scene took place. The bus was not blue but orange and Thomas insisted on wearing a cap exactly like the little boy wore in the picture the teacher had shown him. For parents attempting visual aids for the first time, it can be quite discouraging. An aid, you say? More likely a tantrum instead. Again, it is extremely important to take into account the hyper-selective thought process of people with autism.

Many difficulties occurred during the 'photo period'. Another typical situation was visiting the new swimming pool. Thomas prepared himself as well as possible and to be sure of all the details, I showed

Thomas a picture with a view of the pool and its surroundings. On our arrival, I sensed that Thomas was a bit tense. Then I understood why. To get the photograph, the owner had moved the slide to the one side and then put it back. Thomas had noticed it immediately. He felt he had been mislead.

Schedule with drawings

After all this confusion, it seemed wise to change to a schedule that included drawings. Unfortunately, Thomas seemed to understand very little about drawings. If you look at a drawing of a bicycle or a toothbrush, it looks like a very abstract picture of a bicycle or a toothbrush. For Thomas there seemed to be no connection between the two – photo and drawing.

As we mentioned beforehand, a schedule can be seen as a visual language for people with autism. But again, it is extremely important that they understand the visual information shown, otherwise its use is meaningless. We don't want to be spoken to in Chinese, right? There is often a discrepancy between the things we would like the children to use and what they actually are able to use.

As drawings were still too difficult for Thomas, objects seemed to give him the clearest and most concrete information. This worked without trouble. Some people may see this as regression, a return to the object level, but the important thing was that it worked! Meanwhile, at home and at school, he was doing exercises in sorting, categorising and associating drawing with objects. Thomas began to learn categories and to understand drawings. This was a relief, because I discovered that drawings offered many possibilities and we could avoid all the confusing details.

However, his thinking in details was apparent once in a while even with drawings and one day he became very angry. On one of the drawings in his daily schedule, there were raindrops on the windshield of the bus. But the day Thomas looked at it before taking the bus, it wasn't raining. So again it didn't work, he must have felt that people were telling lies to him once more.

During a training session in Finland, I was responsible for Kaij, a non-verbal teenager with autism. He had a day schedule with drawings, which he used quite independently. Our classroom was in the middle of the woods and I planned for us all to go for a walk every so often.

To explain and make it clear, I drew a small tree on the schedule. But Kaij didn't understand this. He protested when I showed him we were going for a walk. I didn't understand what was going on either, because according to his file, he loved going for walks. During our walk, the answer came to me little by little. The trees were very different from the one I had drawn, and most importantly, they were packed with snow! Kaij did not have the tree-concept and he was stuck in his hyper-selective understanding of the visual perception of a tree, namely the kind of Conifer tree he was used to seeing every day in the woods. My drawing of a fruit tree looked very different indeed.

When I returned to the classroom, I drew a Conifer tree and the next day the change was amazing. When Kaij saw the drawing, he understood immediately that we were going outside.

Many schools use pictograms. I don't think they are bad in themselves, but it often strikes me that in some classrooms all the pupils use the same pictograms. In these classrooms 'visual aid' seems to be synonym for 'use of pictograms.' This is a pity. It is a far cry from the concept of individualisation. Pictograms work well as a visual language for some, but not for everybody. Many people with autism don't understand what they mean.

See for yourself. We have all seen male/female symbols on the doors of toilets and changing rooms. These pictures are a message that you are entering a rest area or a locker room. But ask yourself this, what criteria does a person with autism use to understand this pictogram-symbol? I feel you need to have developed inner concepts about people, objects and activities before you can recognise and understand most pictograms.

Daily schedules with written language

The typeface used for the schedule can also cause problems for the hyper-selective child. Most people with autism who can read and write can deal with different kinds of typeface, but for some children (especially in the beginning) the change from one kind to another can prove quite difficult. From the point of view of a detail thinker, this makes perfect sense.

Breakfast	Breakfast	**Breakfast**	Breakfast
Bus	Bus	**Bus**	Bus
Video	Video	**Video**	Video
Swimming	Swimming	**Swimming**	Swimming
Lunch	Lunch	**Lunch**	Lunch
Bathroom	Bathroom	**Bathroom**	Bathroom
Sleep	Sleep	**Sleep**	Sleep

The Easiest Daily Schedule...a Regression?

A daily schedule can be seen as a kind of visible language for a person with autism and I think it is very important to choose the right kind of daily schedule, one he feels the most comfortable with, even if it is not our ideal. An example: I understand English and French. When I go abroad, I can speak these languages. However, it is a bit of an effort for me. By the time evening comes after a day of speaking French or English, it is relaxing to speak to a colleague in my own language. And yet you couldn't say that either language is over my head.

On weekends and holidays, I often forget Thomas's schedule. Sometimes, he takes care of it by himself. Although he can use written instructions, he will spontaneously go back to old drawings and photos. Some would see this as regression. Personally, I don't think it is the case; it is quite understandable if you take into account the difficulties with perception and with meaning.

First and foremost, the daily schedule should be an aid, one that requires a minimum amount of effort for people with autism. After all, I would never write my agenda in English or French.

During the holidays, Thomas is sometimes allowed to join a group of younger children. He will go and ask Karen, the teacher, if he can also have a schedule with pictures. It makes him very happy. When I say to him, "But Thomas, you can read and write so why do you like photos or drawings so much?" he answers, "Mama, with photos or drawings I see directly what they mean." In other words, he doesn't have to translate them into an easier symbolic code.

Intermezzo issues for parents and siblings only

Some forms of communication are called pre-communication, because they cannot be understood by everyone and because it is difficult to expand them. You work to change 'pre-communication' into a more universal form of communication, towards communication that is understood by everyone. Right?

Yet, I would like to emphasise the enormous emotional importance of some forms of pre-communication for parents and members of the family. If a young child can say only one or two words and these words have a very specific meaning that only his Mum can understand, this can be called pre-communication. Such communication creates a very close relationship. If it seems that no other words are being learned, at least for the time being, does it make sense to get rid of them? We will continue working on alternative kinds of communication, but meanwhile let's not break this closeness.

Thomas speaks fluently and intelligibly. Nevertheless, for him, the 'darling hamper' means something like 'my Mummy loves me dearly'. I am the only one who knows what it means and this could be an example of pre-communication. When I refer to the darling hamper, Thomas knows what I mean. When I have made him very happy, he'll come to me and say, "The darling hamper."

One day, he wanted to have a hamper in his bedroom (he does have his own ideas about gifts). I had a few and I let him select one. He chose one and then asked me if I thought the one he chose was the nicest. I answered, "Yes," immediately and Thomas was overjoyed. "The darling hamper I got from Mum." I was so moved, Thomas seemed so happy, the atmosphere and the whole moment became the darling hamper. Was there any reason to change that? Everyone has their own idiosyncrasies towards people they enjoy being with. Do you get rid of them or do you keep them? Is this really regression?

There is still so much one could write about visual aids, but my purpose here is to show how pervasive the consequences of 'thinking through details' can be, even in the use of daily schedules and various kinds of visual help.

Chapter 5

Teaching Skills and Learning how to Generalise them

"When mother was about to leave, I was terrified. Was she just going to abandon me here? The fact that I had learnt that I was fetched every day from playschool was not something I was able to transfer to this situation. It didn't help me to work out that I would probably be picked up from this strange place too. What had happened in playschool had no relevance here. Everything to do with playschool was in a special compartment in my mind, which could only be opened when I was there, at playschool."

Gunilla Gerland (1998)

It is extremely important to make life as predictable as possible for a person with autism, so he feels that his life is more under control and he develops a positive sense of well being. This is the foundation of all education and teaching.

But children grow up quickly and it is our responsibility, both as parents and professionals, to encourage their independence as much as possible. We teach them the skills they will need most later on: work skills and behaviour, leisure skills, communication and social skills, self-help skills and domestic skills, functional academic skills. While they are learning these new skills, we are often confronted with the consequences of processing information in a hyper-selective way. A few examples will follow. Of course, we mustn't forget the tremendous impact of their difficulties with spontaneous generalisation: just because you can clear the table at school doesn't mean you can do it at home and vice-versa.

"Another consequence of my way of seeing the world was this. It was quite clear to me that a certain object could be lying behind or under another object. If I saw that I understood it, but I connected it only with what I saw. The moment I saw a ball rolling under a bureau, I knew that balls could be found under bureaux. I also realised that the ball was there even when I couldn't see it and I was able to generalise sufficiently to realise that other balls might be concealed by large pieces of furniture. Furthermore, I was able to

add these experiences to my knowledge of the world and apply
them in the future. But they gave me no inkling that there might be
other things besides balls under the bureau or, indeed, that
anything at all might end up under or behind other things so as to
be no longer visible.

My parents mocked and scolded me for my hopeless laziness. The
way it looked from their world was as if I couldn't even be bothered
to lift anything up to search for whatever I was looking for. Had God
ever created a lazier child? Haha."

Gunilla Gerland (1998)

When you have autism, your mind works differently. You do what you can, you check to see if things work, you make concrete associations in order to understand and to give meaning (associations of a specific perceptual detail with another perceptual detail, because a flexible basis of understanding – the 'real' way – is missing): a ladle is always supposed to be in the kitchen, a glass in the bathroom.

Therefore, when the association changes, it may result in incredible tension or tremendous laughter. The association is too rigid in itself and is not flexible enough. The basis for giving meaning, the basis of understanding is inevitably too 'narrow' to allow for spontaneous and flexible generalisations to other contexts. This is the origin of generalisation difficulties in autism. I have heard people with autism call them difficulties with 'automatisation'. How this thinking in details plays a role in the learning process and in the generalisation of skills will be illustrated in the following anecdotes.

Teacher in the classroom, Mum at home

The school bus dropped Thomas off at home every day. But one day there was a parents' meeting at lunchtime, so I told Thomas that I would take him home instead. Thomas seemed very happy and even told the teacher that his Mum would be picking him up. He also mentioned that I would come first and see him at his physical therapy lesson. I was looking forward to it too, mostly because Thomas seemed so thrilled.

When I got to school, Thomas was another person. He was not at all happy; in fact he seemed completely lost. The physical therapist told me that he hadn't done as well as usual. On the way home, and I still don't know how I got him there, he was unmanageable, really naughty. What was going on? Was he as unhappy to see me as it must have seemed to an outsider?

Here again is an example of how people with autism process information differently. Mum is really someone (a detail) who belongs at home (a certain context), not in a classroom, no more than flowers belong on the head of a horse or a ladle in a gymnasium. But if parents don't belong in the classroom, teachers certainly do. But teachers aren't supposed to come to someone's home. I remember the tantrums Thomas threw when his teacher did visit us! She didn't belong in his home. The association was Mum – home, teacher – school. He really 'thought in strict compartments'.

> *"Everyone I didn't know had an empty face, which meant everyone except my family. I didn't realise that these faces were people in the same way as those I knew were people. Those faces were as lacking in content as furniture; and I thought that, just like furniture, they belonged in the rooms I saw them in. I didn't consider them as either children or adults, able to move between different rooms of their own volition – any more than a sofa could. I could go from room to room, I knew that. But if I first saw someone I didn't know in one room and then saw him or her in another, I thought it wasn't the same person. To me the face was empty and there was nothing in it to tell me that I had seen him or her before."*

> Gunilla Gerland (1998)

Many of the stress related issues of people with autism stem from their different way of thinking.

- ◆ Why does Pieter speak with his speech therapist and not with his teacher?
- ◆ Why does Ellen write only with the occupational therapist?
- ◆ Why does Jan only do arithmetic in class?
- ◆ Why does Bart eat soup at school but never at home?
- ◆ Why is Michel toilet-trained at home yet wears Pampers at school?

People who do not understand this 'thinking through details' of people with autism have a tendency to believe that the real issues are laziness or stubbornness.

Here is yet another example of Thomas' hyper-selective understanding of rules. During recess, Thomas was caught pulling grass out of the ground. The teacher told him that pulling grass was not allowed there. Thomas understood immediately. He went 50 yards away and did it again. Was he spoilt? Was he being bad?

> *"The significance of what people said to me, when it sank in as more than just words, was always taken to apply only to that particular moment or situation. Thus, when I once received a serious lecture about writing graffiti on Parliament House during a class trip, I agreed that I'd never do this again and then, ten minutes later, was caught outside writing different graffiti on the school wall. To me, I was not ignoring what I had been told, nor was I trying to be funny; I had not done exactly the same thing as I had done before. My behaviour puzzled others, but theirs puzzled me too. It was not so much that I had no regard for their rules as that I couldn't keep up with the many rules for each specific situation."*

Donna Williams (1996)

So it has nothing to do with unwillingness at all. It's more about having to learn a new set of rules for each and every situation.

> "Likewise, the *'deaf while hearing' phenomenon is related to the small impact occasional remarks have on me. Implicit indirect remarks delivered once only usually don't work. I have experienced that explicit remarks, coming from different persons and expressed in different situations, are bearing the highest meaning-impact. So, for hearing too, consistent meaning-acquisition demands different points of view."*

Van Dalen (1995)

Such hyper-selective thought sometimes becomes extreme. At school, Thomas got his fingers crushed in a door. It must have been very painful. His nails were blue, his fingers flattened. You could see the pain on his face and he had tears in his eyes. He bit his lips not to scream. Anne, a teacher who knows him well, said, "If the pain is that bad you are allowed to cry, you know." Thomas answers, "No, I only cry when I'm with my Mum and sometimes with my sister." Again, spoilt child? Bad boy?

At first glance, it may seem to be the case and it can be difficult for parents to make the people around them understand that it has nothing to do with willfulness or with being stubborn. It may just be impossible, for the time being, for them to 'think' and therefore 'do' otherwise. For children with autism, the spontaneous transfer of skills and behaviour from one context to another can be difficult. The first context might be a person, a location or a combination of the two. Because the context is associated with a detail rather than with its global meaning and they associate specific situations or contexts with specific details, they also link actions and skills specifically to these contexts. If one important detail is missing in another context, they feel lost, even distraught.

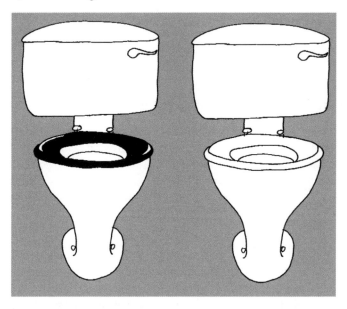

Take Karel's thought process. He is at camp. He does not seem well. Els, his teacher, thinks he needs to use the toilet; it's been days since he has had a bowel movement. She takes him there and nothing happens so she calls Karel's parents, because she is afraid that Karel is ill. She talks to Karel's Mum and explains the situation. Mum asks what colour the toilet seat is. That's a strange question. Els can't remember, so she goes and checks. The answer is white. Well, says Mum, Karel needs a black seat. So, the white seat is covered with black tape. Karel is brought back to the bathroom. When he sees the black seat, he immediately pulls his trousers down and goes. Now he recognises the toilet. His vacation has been saved!

If you think in details and, like Van Dalen, you try to put all the details together, and afterwards notice that a white bowl and a black lid make a toilet and that is where you can relieve yourself, it is hard to believe that a white bowl and a white seat could be used for the same purpose. It certainly was not obvious to Karel.

For a person with autism it goes like this, more or less:

> We say $1 + 2 = 3$
>
> Karel thinks white bowl + black lid = toilet = I can relieve myself.
>
> We would be confused if someone said $1 + 5 = 3$
>
> And Karel was just as confused with:
> white bowl + white toilet seat = toilet.
> What was he supposed to do in that situation?

A different way of thinking, not ill will

So many aspects of daily life that are easy for us may be unexpectedly difficult for people who put so much emphasis on details. Red shoelaces are different from black ones. It's obvious. So you might find someone with autism who can tie red shoelaces, but not black ones. Shoes with 4 holes don't look the same as shoes with 8 holes. So it makes sense that they may find it difficult with one pair and not the other. This also applies to the different ways of closing things like buttons, zippers and Velcro.

Very patiently, Els taught Thomas how to tie shoes using strings on a piece of wood. He finally learned how to do it, but applying the technique to a real shoe in an ordinary situation was not so easy, even though the same technique would be used. People who understand autism know this. There is a big difference between tying a string on the board and your own shoes and it is a huge leap to go from one to the other.

Taking a jacket off is not the same as opening a backpack. Now we can understand a bit better why Klaas can wash his hands at his Mum's and not at his granny's. To draw a parallel, just because you can drive a small sub-compact vehicle, like a Renault Twingo or a Fiat Punto doesn't mean you know how to drive a SUV or a limousine.

Thomas has learnt how to brush his teeth at school. Marleen divided the task into many small steps. Each step was associated with a picture to teach him how to do it. When Thomas had learned how to brush his teeth, he was not able to do it in the classroom, under the supervision of Bert, n teacher. Bert discovered that Thomas would not spit the water out but kept it in his mouth instead. Leaning his head backwards, he would hold the water in, standing as still as a statue, nearly suffocating. Yet Marleen insisted that he could do it perfectly well with her.

She could not figure this new problem out. He had done it all so well before. So she came to the class to show him how to do it one more time. That's when everyone noticed that when Thomas was supposed to spit out the water, she would lightly touch the back of his head and say, "Spit it out." Thomas was waiting for Bert to give him the signal. Thomas had learned tooth brushing as a series of steps, in which each detail was important. Without the slight tap on the head and the words, it wouldn't work.

We notice here that people with autism often develop certain routines as a result of their hyper-selective understanding of activities. It is therefore important to take this into account when you teach them a new skill or else they may become too dependent on a particular detail.

In class, Filip has learned the meaning of wallpaper. When they go into another room, his teacher shows him the wallpaper there and asks him what it is called. Filip does not know. He misses the 'art' of generalisation.

While ordinary children will understand that wallpaper is paper that covers walls, for Filip, it means paper with stripes on it, like the one he has seen in his classroom. He does not spontaneously generalise, because he has only the perception of this one particular wallpaper and not the concept.

A teacher with no specific training in autism might think, "I heard him give the definition of what wallpaper is, I have seen him point at it in the speech therapist's office, so why won't he tell us? What's the matter with him? Does he have a personality problem or is it a different way of thinking?"

> *"I very much wanted to understand and that led me to think up something, a theory about how things worked, that always applied to whatever I saw. Every time my mother came, one thing was always the same: she always came into the hall. What if that meant I had to be in the hall for her to come at all? That's what it was. That must be it, I thought. If she came and I wasn't in the hall, if she didn't see me, would she then go home again? And perhaps it also meant that if I wanted to go home, then she would appear if I*

went out into the hall. I had actually never seen my mother in any other room except the hall, so I associated her appearance with the actual room, as if she just materialised in the doorway. Everything had to hang together in some logical way and now I had probably found it: as long as I was in the hall, the room to which mother always came, then she would come. If on the other hand I was in the wrong room, in any of the rooms into which she never came, then she wouldn't come.

Every moment when I wasn't being watched, I slipped out into the hall and sat on the floor there. It was a better place to be, a calmer place, where I could sit and hope to be fetched sooner."

Gunilla Gerland (1998)

Routines and Situations: The Honeymoon Effect

Many people with autism have tons of routines. In some cases these routines are associated with specific contexts.

One hears remarks such as, "At his Mum's, he taps five times on his chair before sitting, but he doesn't do it at his granny's." If you understand hyper-selectivity, you can imagine that granny's chairs probably don't look like the ones at home and perhaps granny's chairs don't deserve a tap.

Sometimes, when on vacation with their parents and away from home, children with autism will leave some of their difficult behaviour behind. In some cases, taking a child away from his natural environment can help, because he does not spontaneously generalise and apply his previous behaviour to his new environment. Sometimes, you can use the generalisation issue to help him get rid of troublesome behaviour. However, we must remember to include clear and precise visual guides in the new environment or the child will create new routines, which later will be hard to undo. It is worth a try.

When the school bus left in the morning, Thomas would usually wave at me. Sometimes though he wouldn't and I would feel bad. Then I noticed that Thomas waved when the bus was parked on the same side of the street as our house, but he wouldn't wave when the bus was on the opposite side. It had nothing to do with not wanting to wave to me, which was my first reaction. I explained the situation to him and now he waves to me when the bus is on either side. I still need to remind him occasionally when the bus is on the other side. It probably had something to do with the direction in which he was looking.

> "Even though my memories of things are stored as individual specific memories, I am able to modify my mental images. For example, I can imagine a church painted in a different colour or put the steeple of one church onto the roof of another; but when I hear somebody say the word 'steeple', the first church that I see in my imagination is almost always a childhood memory and not a church image that I have manipulated. This ability to modify images in my imagination has helped me to learn how to generalise."

Temple Grandin (1995)

A banana is not a banana

Thomas loves bananas. He takes one to school with him every day. One day, his teacher asked me if Thomas might not prefer to bring in some other kind of fruit, because he had not been eating his banana. Maybe he'd even prefer not to bring any fruit at all. When he got home, Thomas said that the teacher hadn't given him his banana. What happened was that each morning, the teacher would gather up all the children's fruit and then later on would hand it out. Thomas, who knew which banana was his and recognised it in detail, thought that he should be getting his own banana back. In that sense he was quite right. He wasn't getting 'his' banana.

Thomas does not eat bananas at home. I asked him why. Aren't bananas always the same? Thomas says no. At school, bananas are in a school bag. This is true. At home, they are in a fruit bowl and so look different.

So, at home, I put the banana in a school bag and presented it to him and since then he's been eating bananas there too.

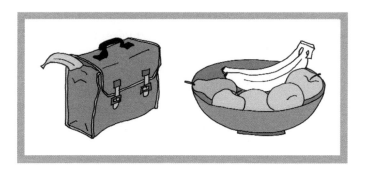

When I mentioned the banana story at a seminar, a mother of another child told me a similar story. Her daughter would only eat bananas with a Chiquita sticker on them. She did not eat any other fruit. Once the Mum understood the hyper-selective thinking mode of her daughter, she started putting Chiquita stickers on all the fruit. Thanks to the Chiquita label, the girl now eats all kinds of fruit.

Thomas would eat soup at his grandmother's, but never at home. I noticed that she would serve it in a special bowl. I bought the same one and since then Thomas eats soup at home too.

You can see here how we can use hyper-selectivity in a positive way. After all, it is a lot better and more pleasant for everyone to work with their thought processes, adapting and remaining positive, rather than imposing change and constantly dealing with behaviour problems. The best way to avoid behavioural issues is to anticipate and prevent them from occurring.

More on food issues and other behaviour and poor education problems

Parents and professionals frequently mention eating difficulties with autistic people. Some eat only a limited variety of foods; others have developed masses of routines. I will not discuss other factors here that may be involved in eating problems, such as sensory issues. I will focus instead on 'thinking through details'.

When Thomas was a little boy, he always wanted the same baby food ('Olvarit' in this case) and it always had to be heated in the same pan. This can happen with ordinary kids too. But with our children, it can grow out of proportion and make things extremely difficult. If an ordinary child is hungry, he recognises food and eats it, even if the packaging is not the same (or in this case the pan). This is not the case for many children with autism. If the packaging (a detail) is different, then everything is different. To outsiders these children may appear spoiled. I think we should respect their thought process by using it to help them become more flexible. It's important to remember that they're not doing it to annoy us. We can't expect them to switch to our way of thinking from one moment to the next.

Let's try to see through the eyes of a person with autism. We tell Geert, a boy with autism, that he's going to have chicken. Geert understands a number of words and the word chicken is definitely one of them. At lunchtime, he gets angry. Weren't we supposed to be having chicken? For him, there is a big difference between what his teacher has taught him to call chicken, on the farm and at home and what is on his plate today.

Suppose you have been told to go and buy a chicken. The appearance of chicken sold in supermarkets also varies, regardless of the packaging.

One day, Thomas saw a chicken being plucked before being packaged. As one of the first steps in chicken-recognition, I always gave him a thigh to eat as, from a perceptual point of view, it's the piece that is the most recognisable in the shop. The picture of a chicken is quite different from the one you eat or from the one on your plate or from the thing you buy in the shop...

Intermediate steps, pros and cons

In the park next to our house, there is a big birdhouse with some beautiful birds and some chickens. Thomas and I went for a walk and noticed a class of small children gathered around the birdcage. When Thomas saw the chickens, he said aloud, "Chickens! We'll eat them all and first we'll pluck their feathers." The children looked at him in shock. Yet he is really a sweet little boy.

Moreover, food can be cooked in many ways and so can look different. There is no iconic relationship anymore between one dish and another. For example, we eat a lot of turkey. If you look at it from a hyper-selective point of view, there is a big difference between a roast, a slice on a sandwich and a turkey potpie.

During another walk, we saw some children surrounding a cage with a rabbit. Thomas went to look at them and asked, "Are we going to eat it?" The kids looked at him in horror. But for Thomas, things are different. Now at least he sees a real rabbit, because the rabbit on our plate is so different. The rabbit we serve on a dish or in a sauce has nothing to do with the animal in the cage.

Thomas always eats his food separately on his plate at home and many parents have similar experiences with their autistic children. When he was little, he refused to eat his potatoes if there was a bit of gravy on them. He wouldn't eat his meat if it were covered with vegetables. So a plate with dividers seems to be a good solution. Now that he can talk, he can explain his reasons for doing so, "Otherwise, you can't be sure they are potatoes." The same goes for spinach. He always wants it in butter sauce. And although he loves them both, he eats them separately. "If not, I can't tell if it is spinach or not."

"And now, let's have an egg." As far as Thomas is concerned, he only eats boiled eggs, because at least they look like the real thing! It was quite an ordeal to get him to eat a boiled egg in an eggcup. He calls it 'an egg in a cup' and he always wants the same eggcup. If you look at a fried egg and a scrambled egg, there is no similarity between them and an egg. Thomas calls a fried egg 'an egg in the pan'. He doesn't like them. So, when he is very cross with someone he says, 'I'll ask Mum to prepare 'an egg in the pan' for you!'

There is also a big difference between a fish that has just come out of the sea or a river and one you have cooked. For Thomas, a trout stands for fish, so I began by serving him trout. He ate it with no problems.

I was a bit uneasy seeing him always start with the eyes. They had to be there. What was a fish without eyes? I had to get rid of the head and tail very quickly so that he didn't eat them too. Thank goodness, he let me take them away. I had to be very cunning because the head and the tail had to be on the plate as long as possible or it didn't look like a fish. In the beginning, I also had to call the fish 'naughty', to persuade him to eat it. Then he felt mighty, because he had defeated the naughty fish.

For my next step, I put the fish on the table whole and then cut it, so he could see it was really a fish. Little by little, we put a slice of lemon on each piece of the naughty fish, except for Thomas' piece, because you either eat fish or lemon. The head and the tail had to remain on the table so that we could be sure it was a fish we were having. And over and over, we had to say it was a naughty fish.

My next step was to get Thomas to eat a piece of fish that didn't look like a fish, but he still needed visual help or he wouldn't eat it. I put a picture of a trout on the table (from a frozen box) for him to look at once in a while so he could be sure he was eating the naughty fish. For him, this was an important step. I was impressed and moved. I was also amazed because I saw that he was doing his best despite his problems. It was not easy for him. People with autism must make more of an effort than we can imagine. I think we would probably prefer, in the same circumstances, to just always eat the same thing.

The Ice Cream Drama

Thomas's three all-time favourite flavours are pistachio, strawberry and orange.

When we went down town one day, I promised him that we'd go and get an ice cream. I knew a lovely place opposite his favourite streetcar stop. The tramway made sounds he liked and I thought this would be an excellent opportunity to work on his eating out habits. I would always put him in a corner so he wouldn't be able to run away. I also looked for armchairs and tried to select a spot conducive to watching and listening. Once we had settled down I ordered ice cream in his favourite flavours.

The ice cream came in a glass bowl and looked very different from the one in the cone that he was used to. Thomas had been prepared beforehand, so he knew that ice cream didn't always look the same. I felt comfortable.

Perhaps I was being over-confident so I took him back to town the following week. Thomas was excited and so was I. I wasn't used to something working out quite so quickly, with so little preparation. We settled down in the same place. Although Thomas himself said, "You shouldn't always choose the same thing," he ordered the same ice cream.

We got the ice cream right, but this time it was a failure. The green scoop had to be on the bottom, the orange in the middle and the pink on top. I told him that it made no difference but he didn't agree at all. To my dissatisfaction, Thomas struggled to get the green ball, which was in the middle, to the bottom, and the orange down to the middle, and the pink one from the bottom to the top. Meanwhile the ice cream was melting and spilling onto the table, his sweater and his legs. People were staring at us, looking horrified. Thomas got angrier and angrier at the ice cream, which was turning into syrup and with the 'dumb waiter' who should have known better and dished the scoops out in the right order. I ended up leaving with Thomas furious and strangers staring and making the usual comments about badly brought up children and the lack of discipline these days.

I thought the situation through and when I understood what had happened, I tried again a few weeks later. I told Thomas that I'd tell the dumb waiter how he should prepare the ice cream. He in turn should address him as 'Sir', not speak too loud, eat nicely, etc…To be on the safe side, I wrote down our agreement just in case.

I ordered the ice cream and insisted on the order in which it should be scooped: first, the green on the bottom (according to him, on the bottom is not the same as underneath), then the orange in the middle (for him that's not the same as in between) and finally, the pink on top (not above, as you may have guessed). I explained how important it was to the waiter and he left smiling, full of good intentions. A few minutes later, he came back with the ice cream. To be nice, he had added small umbrellas to make it look pretty and moreover, multi-coloured sprinkles.

Needless to say, Thomas was very upset. The first thing he did was to take off all the trimmings and try to pick out all the small sprinkles, an impossible task. Like the previous time, it was a disaster and it ended with a tantrum. The nice waiter didn't know what had happened. What was he supposed to think about it?

Months later, Freek, Thomas' brother, told me why Thomas wanted his ice cream scoops in that order – to be like a traffic light: green, orange and red! This order had to be respected, period.

For all those parents who are criticised for their child's lack of discipline or for how difficult their autistic child is, here is a poem for you, by way of a consolation prize.

Peter and Polly

Do dirty things in the kindergarten yard

They are little pigs

The other toddlers stare at them

And Mrs Teacher looks at them too

Oh! What big pigs they are

She takes a piece of paper and a fountain pen

And writes, in anger:

Dear parents,

Next time please produce better children

And the parent's reply: Dear Mrs Teacher,

We are constantly getting married and getting divorced

We are experimenting with different kinds of children.

Sandor Weöres, on little boys

Detail Thinking can also Influence Academic Achievement

Colour the long objects in red and the short ones in green. In this exercise, Thomas did not look at each item as a whole. For the train, he saw immediately, with meticulous precision, that some carriages were smaller than others.

Counting

1 + 1 = 2
2 + 2 = 4
3 + 4 = 7
5 + 4 = 9
6 + 3 = 9
4 + 5 = 9

- - - - - - - - - - - - - - - - - -

1 + 1 = 2		5 + 4 = 9
2 + 2 = 4		6 + 3 = 9
3 + 4 = 7		4 + 5 = 9

When I introduced a different layout with two columns, Thomas was no longer able to add. I had to cover one column for him. With some children of a lower developmental level, I have noticed that you have to be careful not to give them too much information at one time. It may be helpful to cover part of the task or the work (e.g. with puzzles or beads).

Meanwhile, Thomas learned to generalise. He can now work with two columns. One day he seemed to have done his homework too quickly. When I asked him if he had finished it, he replied that it was done. In his way of thinking, he was right. There was a dot missing (look at 13 + 4=) and he had filled it in. So for him, the homework had been done.

17 - 6 = ...	16 + 4 = ...
12 + 4 = ...	12 - 1 = ...
19 - 7 = ...	16 - 3 = ...
13 + 4 = ..	14 + 4 = ...
16 - 6 = ...	17 - 2 = ...
17 - 3 = ...	20 - 3 = ...
20 + 0 = ...	17 + 1 = ...

The transition from capital letters to small letters and then to cursive writing was, for Thomas, strictly associated with the person who had taught him. Later on he associated each type of writing with the paper on which he wrote it: block letters on paper without lines, cursive on paper with lines. It was a bit of a problem, but by making the lines thinner and thinner until they were hardly visible, Thomas finally did generalise to writing cursive on a piece of plain paper. Here the important contextual detail was a person or a piece of paper.

In order to generalise skills, it is crucial to work on broadening the context. It is essential that professionals work closely with parents in order to achieve this.

Other Issues that Involve Detail Thinking

In two articles, Van Dalen mentions some serious consequences of 'thinking through details'. I will summarise them for you, adding my comments here and there. The reader is welcome to read the entire documents published in Engagement, a publication of the Dutch Autism Association (NVA – Nederlandse Vereniging Autisme).

Consequences

1. Nothing is ever the same.
It is true that details often change. Therefore we can understand why people with autism have such a need for things being the same (even a need for stereotypical behaviour).

2. Time goes by faster for them.
While we may think they are being slow, they themselves may think they are working everything out very quickly (they have so much information and so many more details to process, details we don't even notice so we don't need as much time to deal with them).

3. 'Thinking through details' has an impact on spatial perception.
If you are in a small space, you have fewer details to deal with than in a large one. Therefore many people with autism prefer small places.

Consequences such as these should not be seen as strict rules. Some of these consequences seem very important, but let's not forget the principles of individualised suggestions. Let's take into account the 'potential' consequences.

For Thomas, it is very important to have spaces without much stimulation. I remember once having to take all unnecessary decoration, e.g. cups, saucers and vases, to the attic to avoid them being thrown onto the floor. For him to work successfully at school, a stimuli-free area was best.

On the other hand, I noticed that his bedroom is cluttered with all kinds of things. Each item has a specific place and he hates having his room cleaned. From his point of view, of course, it makes perfect sense. If everything is arranged according to our ideas or norms, then he has to use his thought power to put everything back into place. He associates all the activities with specific arrangements in his room.

An example: Thomas goes into his room and finds his brother Jeroen playing with his Nintendo. He yells, "You should be ashamed of yourself! You should be ashamed of yourself! When you play with my Nintendo, you have to turn on the orange lamp. The white lamp has to be on the floor, the desk chair set this way. The luminous cat must be plugged in and the little light above my bed has got to be on!"

> "Sometimes I think I would save a lot of energy if I lived in a smaller place. It would be more intimate. There would be no staircase between the various rooms. Yes, everything you do, you have to do over and over. I often go up and down the stairs ten times and there is still no click in my mind to tell me what I was meant to be doing in the first place. When I'm very tired, it happens frequently."

Gerrie, talking to Suzan and Annie van Keymeulen, A (1995)

4. Anxiety

It takes time to construct things (i.e. to put the details together), whether it regards people, objects or situations.

> "...my first encounter with a physical object is a partial one. The experience of fear due to partial perception can best be understood by referring to a confrontation with a silhouette in the dark: one knows that something is there but it is not altogether immediately clear what it is."

> Van Dalen (1995)

Only later on can you be sure that there is no danger.

5.

> "...I like to compare autistical eyes with the facet-eye of an insect. There are many subtle different details but they are unintegrated."

> Van Dalen (1995)

People's faces don't seem to be well integrated. Gunilla Gerland thought that behind their façade, houses were empty, hollow. Some people with autism have the same impression about people. Behind the faces, the façades, there is nothing.

6. Generalisation issues.

This has been discussed on page 74. Gunilla Gerland calls it her problems with 'automatisation', personal communication.

7. Seeing and meaning

Each and every time, it is a struggle to make the translation from perception to meaning. People with autism need time to process the information received. Let's go back to the many steps Van Dalen has to go through to recognise a hammer.

First, he looks at all the different parts.

Second, he puts them together.

Third, he finds the word used to identify the thing.

Then, he understands its use – you can hammer with it.

Gunilla Gerland talks about her interest in cranes. She first sees their components and shape. Only afterwards does she see their function. The perception process happens little by little and not always automatically. So this kind of perception too requires an amazing amount of effort for people with autism.

People with autism who look at their daily schedule may seem to spend too much time doing so. In fact they actually may need more time. They need time to recognise the picture, drawing, object or word and to absorb all the details included in their program. It requires a great deal of energy to process the information and understand it. Once they have, they can go ahead and do what is planned.

> "Autistic persons are known to be 'blind while seeing' and 'deaf while hearing'. So am I. The 'blind while seeing' phenomenon has to do with the fact that because of my over-selectivity I do not grasp immediately the full meaning inherent to the perception of the totality of an object. The acquisition of the full meaning requires some observation time from different points of view. It is particularly difficult to communicate to non-autistics this phenomenon because for them perception is implicit and immediate. For them, the gap between first object – impression and final meaning – acquisition is almost neglectable in comparison with autistics."

> Van Dalen (1995)

The Value of Patience

With Thomas, this is particularly true for spoken language. When you ask him something, he seems at first not to have heard. To get his attention, it is best first to call him by his given name.

The information eventually gets through, little by little, and after a while, longer than with most ordinary children, the information is received. Often, Thomas whispers the request back. Once he has, you know he has received the message and you see that he realises that he has been asked something. Afterwards, he then acts on it. Sometimes, we compare this process with a coin machine – the penny has finally dropped.

When Thomas tells us a joke, he always does so literally and includes all the details. If we interrupt him to say that we've heard it already, he has to start all over again from the beginning.

> "I noticed once the following with respect to delayed action. In my familiar environment a birdhouse had been blown down by a gust of wind. Accidentally passing by nearby, I did not see anything peculiar except for a feeling that 'something is wrong'. (This warning-signal was closely related to this diffused fear I mentioned before.)

After that, I saw, like the case with the hammer, a configuration inter-connectedness of all these parts, where after in the next moment, a name could be attached to all of it: that of a 'birdhouse'! Until then, I still had not realised its miserable status, the restoring action was performed a moment later when I had grasped the full meaning of the scene..."

Van Dalen (1994)

"...Before taken proper action, autistic people must go through a number of separate stages in perception by making 'decisions'. It is very important to realise that, if this long decision-chain is interrupted by the outside world, the autistic person must start all over again because over-selectivity has changed the scene completely. In other words, an interruption effectively wipes away any intermediate result confronting the autistic person literally 'for the first time' with the fallen birdhouse..."

Van Dalen (1994)

"My mind is like a CD-ROM in a computer – like a quick-access videotape. But once I get there, I have to play that whole part."

Temple Grandin in Sacks (1995)

8. Repetitive behaviour.
Each and every time, if there is an interruption in the long chain of decisions in the long sequence of the perception cycle (from initial perception to understanding), you must always start again from the beginning. This is why it is better to do one thing at a time, one thing after another, rather than doing many things at the same time. Each new element requires, as always, lots of different steps and rehearsals to be grasped, instead of an immediate intake. Constant repetition can be proof of a dead end situation.

9. Perception processes break down, especially in social situations. The latter are also the most demanding. "This is when I really feel most easily burned out."

10. Normal people are multi-tracked.
People with autism are mono-tracked. They can either see or do, but rather not both at the same time. It requires such an effort that in some cases, it can bring them to the point of exhaustion. We should not think that Thomas is lazy when he says, "I am too tired to speak" or "Thinking makes me so tired."

11. Making a choice is much more difficult.
Over-selectivity, the multitude of details involved in each of the numerous steps and the intermediate decisions that have to be made remind us of choice-processes.

12. Cause and effect.
Because there are so many possibilities, it is not always easy to be sure of cause and effect in a relationship. Take a dried up plant for instance. To most people it will be obvious that it has dried out because it has not been watered. But for people with autism simple reality may not be so easy to understand. They may wonder whether this phenomenon will cause something terrible to happen or think it is the result of something else that happened before.

13. Coincidence.
If you fully understand point 12, then you can imagine that, in the life of a person with autism, many things seem to be dominated by coincidence.

How can you tell if the situation has been assessed correctly? In a new situation Thomas always thinks up a multitude of possibilities in advance. His frequent questioning illustrates the point.

At the airport, he'll hear a dog barking and say:

> "Mum, is the dog little or big?"
>
> "Will it bite me? What does it look like?"
>
> "Is it on a leash or is it running free?"
>
> "It's in a cage, Thomas."
>
> "Can it get out?"
>
> "Can it bite through the bars?"
>
> "If it sees me, will it jump on me?"
>
> "If it gets out, will it come and bite me?"
>
> "What do I do if it begins to run away?"
>
> "Can it run faster than me?"
>
> "What will you do if it jumps on me?"

Because of his 'thinking through details', he thinks of all the possibilities. You can understand how difficult this can be in social situations.

Donna Williams (1996) tells us the following story in which she ironically speaks of her reaction to a sleeping dog. When a gifted person with autism read it, she burst out laughing and said, "Yes that's it. This is exactly the way I deal with information."

The condition of 'the dog that wouldn't move'

The what? (The condition)
   canine inability to move.

The how? (The symptoms)
   dog appears unable to move from one place to another.

The why? (The cause)
   dog is glued to the floor
   dog is dead
   dog is made of wood
   dog is asleep.

The when/where/who (or solutions):
   unglue the dog
   bury dead dog and get one which does move
   stick wheels on the feet of the wooden dog
   wait till dog wakes up.

There are so many possibilities; any one of them seems (almost) possible.

When we were visiting a zoo someone said, "Look, there is a red panda in the tree!" All the children looked up. Thomas did too. There was indeed a panda, and everyone saw it, everyone except Thomas. How could that be? We all laughed. "Come on, Thomas, why can't you see the red panda?" Thomas replied, "You shouldn't make fun of me. Panda is a brand of Fiat and it is a good brand of car. Red is my favourite colour. I don't see a red panda in the tree." A car in a tree? Completely surrealistic, but for someone with autism nothing is impossible.

14. If you have grasped the importance of the last two points, then this consequence should be crystal clear. In an environment adapted to autism many of the possible superfluous details and choices have already been taken away and therefore meaning becomes more easily accessible.

There exists a strong parallel between an artist or creative scientist and a person with autism. Artists and people with autism need a certain amount of protection for their top performances and their environment should respect this.

   "The creativity of the artist or the scientist results in abstract
   objects like pictures, sculptures or consistent scientific theories, etc.

The creativity of an autist, however, results in the meaningful perception of a physical object, like a hammer or a birdhouse. An autist, therefore, is continuously involved in creative work, most efforts producing incomplete pieces of art but occasionally producing a piece of masterwork."

With many thanks to J.G.T. Van Dalen

Afterword

In the 17th Century, Locke believed, but not for long, in an impossible language in which each thing separately, each stone, each bird and each branch would have its own name. At one point in time, Funes thought of an identical language, but gave it up because it seemed too general and not precise enough.

Indeed, Funes remembered not only each leaf of each tree, of each mountain, but also each time he had seem them in reality or in his imagination. He decided to limit his daily writings about the past and to only keep seventy thousand memories that he would express, later on, in numbers.

Two considerations prevented him from executing his project: the realisation that the work had no limits and that it was useless. He understood that at the time of his death, he would not even have finished the part on all his childhood memories.

The two projects just mentioned (a vocabulary without boundaries for the usual sequence of numbers, a useless mental register of pictures and memories) have no meaning, but show a kind of shaky grandeur.

It allows us to guess or presume what the dizzy/giddy world of Funes could have been. We must remember that he was nearly incapable of having platonic and general ideas.

It was not easy for him to understand that the dog species included different sizes and shapes. It disturbed him that the 3:14 p.m. dog, the one seen sideways, had the same name as the 3:15 p.m. dog, the one seen facing him.

I would imagine that each word I had uttered and each movement I had made would survive in his ruthless mind. I couldn't move for fear of making purposeless gestures.

Jorge Luis Borges, The Ruthless Mind of Funes (1964)

Bibliography

Bruner, J. (1974) Beyond the Information Given, George Allen and Unwin Ltd.

Borges, J.L. (1964) Funes the Memorious. In: Labyrinths. Irby, Donald I. Yates & James E.

Dawson, G. (Ed) (1989) Autism: Nature, diagnosis and treatment, London, The Guilford Press.

Frith, U. (1989) Autism. Explaining the Enigma., Oxford, Basil Blackwell.

Gerland, G. (1996) A Real Person. Life on the Outside, Souvenir Press.

Grandin, T. (1995) Thinking in Pictures, New York, Doubleday.

Hermelin, B. & O'Connor, N. (1970) Psychological Experiments with Autistic Children, Oxford, Permon Press.

Hermelin, B. (1978) Images and Language. In: Rutter, M. & Schopler, E. Autism. A Reappraisal of Concepts and Treatment, New York, Plenum Press.

Hobson, R.P. (1989) Beyond Cognition. A Theory of Autism. In: Dawson, G. (Ed) Autism. Nature, Diagnosis and Treatment, London, The Guilford Press.

Joliffe, Th., Lansdown, R. & Robinson, C. (1992) Autism. A Personal Account. Communication, 26, 3.

Klinger, L. & Dawson, G. (1995) A Fresh Look At Categorisation Abilities In Persons With Autism. In: Schopler, E. & Mesibov, G. (Eds) Learning and Cognition, New York, Plenum Press.

Lovaas, O.I., Koegel, R.L. & Schreibman, L. (1979) Stimulus Over-selectivity in Autism. Psychological Bulletin, 86, 6 (Also in Cook, A.R., Anderson, N. & Rincover, A. & Egel, A. (Eds) Educating and Understanding Autistic Children, College Hill Press, San Diego.)

Menyuk, P. & Quill, K. (1985) Semantic Problems in Autistic Children. In: Schopler, E. en Mesibov, G. (Eds), Communication Problems in Autism, New York, Plenum Press.

Messer, D. (1995) The Development Of Communication, New York, Wiley.

Peeters, T. (1986) De Gevolgen van Autisme op het Gezinsleven. In: Autisme en Gezin. Gent, VVA-congres.

Peeters, T. (1997) From Theoretical Understanding To Educational Intervention, Whurr Publishers Ltd.

Piaget, J. (1959, 1971) The Language and Thought of the Child, New York, Routledge & Kegan Paul, Ltd.

Queiroz, C. (1996) Theater Van De Pop. In: Stassijns, K., Van Strijtem, I. De Mooiste van de Hele Wereld, Tielt, Lannoo.

Rutter, M. & Schopler, E. (1987) Autism And Developmental Disorders. Concepts And Diagnostic Issues. In: Journal of Developmental Disorders, 17, 59.

Rosch, E. (1973) Principles of Categorisation. In: Rosch, E. (Ed) Cognition and Categorisation, Hillsdale, Erlbaum.

Sacks, O. (1995) Een Antropoloog op Mars, Meulenhoff/Kritak, Amsterdam.

Schuler, A. & Borman, (1980) Emerging Language In Autistic Children. In: Fay & Schuler, University Park Press.

Schuler, A. & Prizant, B. (1986) Echolalia. In: Schopler, E. & Mesibov, G. (Eds) Communication Problems in Autism, New York, Plenum Press.

Van Dalen, J.G.T. (1994) Autism from Within. In: Link, Autism Europe, 3rd quarter, 1995, Nr. 17, p. 11.

Van Der Veer, R. & Valsiner, J. (1994) The Vygotsky Reader, Basil, Oxford, Blackwell Ltd.

Van Keymeulen, A. (1995) Ik ben Mijn Eigen Mens., Epo.

Verpoorten, R. (1997) Kwalitatieve Stoornissen In De Waarneming. In-Service, Opleidingscentrum Autisme, Malle.

Weores, S. (1995) Vers Gaat Vreemd. In: Heyman, E., Stassijns, K. & Van Strijtem, I., Standaard Uitgeverij, Antwerpen.

Williams, D. (1996) Autism. An Inside-Out Approach, London, Jessica Kingslcy.

Wing, L. (1976) Early Childhood Autism: Clinical, Educational and Social Aspects. Pergamon

Lucky Duck is more than a publishing house and training agency. George Robinson and Barbara Maines founded the company in the 1980's when they worked together as a head and psychologist developing innovative strategies to support challenging students.

They have an international reputation for their work on bullying, self-esteem, emotional literacy and many other subjects of interest to the world of education.

George and Barbara have set up a regular news-spot on the website. Twice yearly these items will be printed as a newsletter. If you would like to go on the mailing list to receive this then please contact us:

website: www.luckyduck.co.uk

e-mail: newsletter@luckyduck.co.uk

Don't forget to visit our website for all our latest publications, news and reviews.

www.luckyduck.co.uk

New publications every year on our specialist topics:

▸ **Emotional Literacy**

▸ **Self-esteem**

▸ **Bullying**

▸ **Positive Behaviour Management**

▸ **Circle Time**

▸ **Anger Management**

▸ **Asperger's Syndrome**

▸ **Eating Disorders**

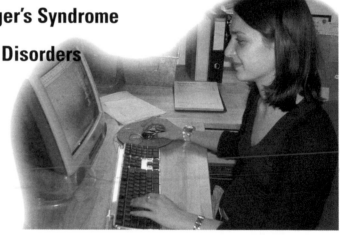